The Psychopathology of Political Ideologies

Inspired by Freud's *The Psychopathology of Everyday Life*, this book examines the unconscious processes shaping contemporary political ideologies.

Addressing ten fundamental questions, Robert Samuels identifies four basic political ideologies: liberal, conservative, Left, and Right, which are often placed in the structure of a logical square, determined by two binary oppositions, with a fifth structure of centrism complicating the square. He turns to psychoanalysis to explain the unconscious defense mechanisms that structure these political ideologies. Each chapter uses a recent, influential title as a gateway to the analysis of the ideologies and structures identified. Through this analysis, Samuels argues that belief in ideological structures is tied to the triumvirates of institutions and ideals; conservatives are tied to premodern institutions of religion, feudalism, and monarchy, while modern liberals are tied to ideals of universality, objectivity, and empiricism. He concludes that this investment in universality shapes the ethics of modern globalization and democratic liberalism. Unlike other books, conclusions are reinforced through examples drawn from current events with an integrated model of different psychopathologies.

The Psychopathology of Political Ideologies moves beyond providing an understanding of what drives different political investments, to offer a more rational and conscious comprehension of subjectivity and social organization. This book will be a great resource for those interested in politics, political science psychology, social psychology, globalization, and ideology.

Robert Samuels is a lecturer of writing at the University of California, Santa Barbara. He is the author of numerous books, including *Teaching Writing, Rhetoric, and Reason at the Globalizing University* (2021).

Psychoanalytic Political Theory

Edited by Matthew H. Bowker, Medaille College and David W. McIvor, Colorado State University

Psychoanalytic Political Theory provides a publishing space for the highest quality scholarship at the intersection of psychoanalysis and normative political theory. It offers a forum for texts that deepen our understanding of the complex relationships between the world of politics and the world of the psyche.

Recently Published Books

The Lucid Vigil
Deconstruction, Desire and the Politics of Critique
Stella Gaon

Individuality and Ideology in British Object Relations Theory
Gal Gerson

The Psychopathology of Political Ideologies
Robert Samuels

Psychoanalysis Under Occupation
Practicing Resistance in Palestine
Stephen Sheehi and Lara Sheehi

For more information about this series, please visit: www.routledge.com/Psychoanalytic-Political-Theory/book-series/PPT

The Psychopathology of Political Ideologies

Robert Samuels

Routledge
Taylor & Francis Group
NEW YORK AND LONDON

First published 2022
by Routledge
605 Third Avenue, New York, NY 10158

and by Routledge
2 Park Square, Milton Park, Abingdon, Oxon, OX14 4RN

Routledge is an imprint of the Taylor & Francis Group, an informa business

Library of Congress Cataloging-in-Publication Data
A catalog record for this title has been requested

ISBN: 978-1-032-05883-2 (hbk)
ISBN: 978-1-032-05882-5 (pbk)
ISBN: 978-1-003-19964-9 (ebk)

DOI: 10.4324/9781003199649

Typeset in Times New Roman
by Deanta Global Publishing Services, Chennai, India

To the memory of Jacqueline Samuels

Contents

1 Introduction

Inspired by Freud's *The Psychopathology of Everyday Life*, this book examines the unconscious processes shaping contemporary political ideologies.[1] The goal here is not only to understand what drives different political investments and structures but to also provide a more rational and conscious comprehension of subjectivity and social organization. By making unconscious formation conscious, this model of political analysis reveals the roots of conservative, liberal, Left-wing, Right-wing, and centrist ideologies. Thus, instead of seeing our political choices as defined by a strict polarization, I seek to differentiate among five specific political psychopathologies.

To help define the ideologies dominant in the United States and other parts of the world, I offer in Chapter Two a critical analysis of Jonathan Haidt's *The Righteous Mind*.[2] I turn to this book because it also presents five specific political belief systems, but his reliance on evolutionary psychology prevents him from taking a psychoanalytic perspective on political psychopathologies. Moreover, through its commitment to biological determinism, his work unintentionally feeds a Right-wing backlash discourse.[3]

Chapter Three examines Ezra Klein's *Why We're Polarized* to determine how our political culture and our everyday lifestyle choices appear to be so divided and opposed.[4] One of my central arguments is that Klein's text is itself an example of polarized thinking as it tries to translate the five basic political ideologies into the simple opposition of Republican versus Democrat. This polarizing perspective is in part due to his reliance on social science research that often unknowingly frames its experiments and findings through an oppositional structure; instead of being aware of its own biases and preconceptions, this research on polarization re-enacts what it is trying to discover.

DOI: 10.4324/9781003199649-1

In Chapter Four, I look at Corey Robin's *The Reactionary Mind: Conservatism from Edmund Burke to Sarah Palin* to analyze why the contemporary Right is often so misunderstood.[5] By offering Freud's theory of perversion as a model for libertarian thinking, I clarify the distinction between conservatives and the Right. What is so interesting about Robin's book is that in his effort to trace the intellectual roots of contemporary Republican politics, he ends up further mystifying the content of this political ideology.

Chapter Five moves from a look at the Right to an examination of the contemporary Left. In reading Robin DiAngelo's *White Fragility*, I show that her insightful critique of progressive racism and liberal defensiveness is coupled with the use of a Left-wing rhetoric centered on making others feel guilt and shame for their words and thoughts.[6] Through the use of the unconscious processes of denial, splitting, and projection, DiAngelo helps us understand some of the problematic aspects of contemporary Leftist thought and politics.

Chapter Six turns to Anthony Pagden's *The Enlightenment: and Why It Still Matters* to examine the relation between psychoanalysis and modern liberal ideology.[7] In looking at the roots of science, democracy, and capitalism, I argue that we need to defend the anti-ideology ideology of modernity. This discourse of critical introspection is then tied to Freud's invention of analytic neutrality and free association.[8]

Theoretical Introduction: Understanding Political Ideologies

I argue in this book that throughout the world, we often find four basic political ideologies: liberal, conservative, Left, and Right.[9] These ideologies can be placed in the structure of a logical square determined by two binary oppositions:

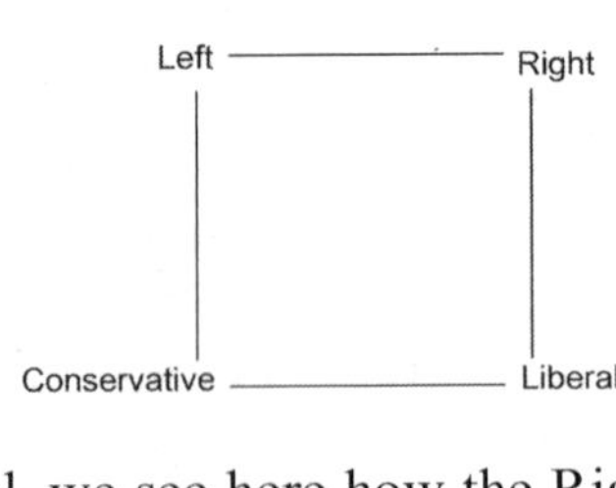

On the most basic level, we see here how the Right is defined in opposition to the Left, and liberalism is defined in opposition to conservativism. However, this structure is complicated by the way that contemporary liberals are much different from modern liberals, and so it is necessary to add a fifth ideology, centrism to the structure:

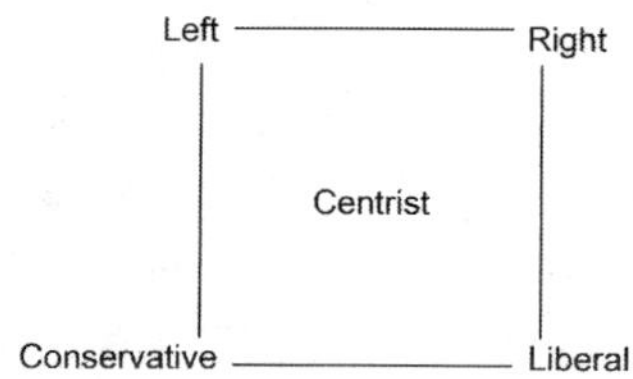

As I will demonstrate, we should not think of centrists as a neutral middle-ground because they have their own psychopathology that distorts their view of themselves and the world.[10]

Starting with conservative ideology, this belief system still structures many of the cultural oppositions that shape our social systems. On the most basic level, this discourse is tied to the premodern focus on a predetermined social hierarchy internalized through a process of unconscious identification and masochistic submission producing the three central premodern institutions of religion, feudalism, and monarchy.[11] In contrast, what in part defines modern liberalism is the invention of three alternative institutions: science, capitalism, and democracy:

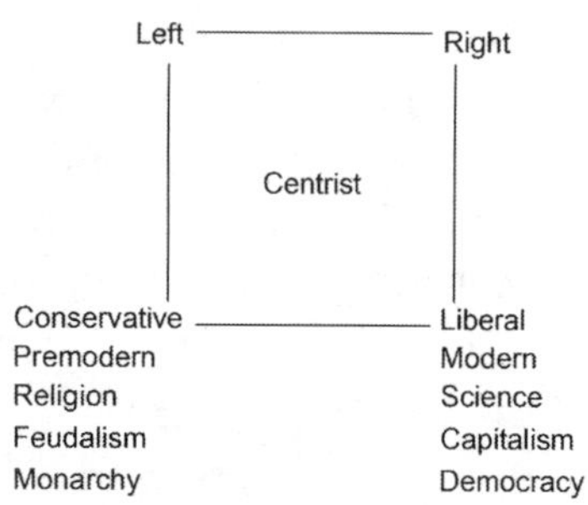

While premodern subjectivity is dominated by faith, belief, and the acceptance of a naturalized social hierarchy, the modern subject is supposed to use reason in a neutral way to determine the truth about empirical reality. Moreover, modernity itself is determined by the necessary but impossible ideals of universality, objectivity, and empiricism.[12] According to this structure, the modern liberal subject must use the reality principle to move beyond the biases derived from the premodern order. I argue that this investment in universality shapes the ethics of globalization and modern democratic liberalism.[13]

In response to premodern conservatives and modern liberals, we find Left-wing ideology that is centered on a hysterical identification with suffering and the use of a victim-based fantasy structure to influence others on an emotional level.[14] Part of this ideology is determined by a desire to reverse the social hierarchies shaping premodern culture. For instance, instead of men dominating women, women seek to gain more social power. The postmodern period is then shaped by minority-based social movements seeking to expand the modern system of democratic justice, but as we will see, these movements often become fixated on a particular group identity. Since in order to promote in-group solidarity, it is necessary to draw a clear distinction between the good "us" and the evil "other," this type of political polarization tends to create an ideology centered on the conflict between the pure and innocent victim and the evil perpetrator. Moreover, in this structure, the victim's vengeance is always justified, and the victim cannot be criticized or questioned, and so this group psychopathology makes it difficult to resolve conflicts and embrace the modern ideals of neutrality, objectivity, and universality.[15]

In response to Left-wing politics, we are witnessing the rise of Right-wing ideology. A key aspect of this psychopathology is a stress on the freedom of the competitive individual who resists being shamed and censored by the politically correct Leftist super-ego.[16] Through a combination of perversion, sociopathy, and borderline personality structures, the Right-wing libertarian expresses impulses without shame or guilt using the unconscious processes of denial, splitting, and projection.[17] Furthermore, the Right often takes on its own victim identification by reversing the postmodern reversal of premodern social hierarchies. In a dialectical structure, the Left seeks to overcome conservative prejudices, and the Right then strives to overcome the Left's social movements and censorship.

In response to the Left and the Right, we find the centrist compromise, which itself is structured by a narcissistic and obsessional psychopathology.[18] Since the narcissist wants to have its ideal ego validated by others, it often signals its moral virtues by accepting the moralism of the Left, and yet these obsessional centrists want to maintain the status quo, and so they seek out slow reforms instead of the revolutions demanded by the Left. These centrists also tend to see the political world in a polarized way as they gain a sense of moral superiority by laughing at the "insanity" of the Right.

I realize that some people will be turned off by this effort to pathologize political ideologies and different groups of people; however, I believe that it is necessary to look at politics from a psychoanalytic perspective because much of the social and subjective processes are irrational, unconscious, and unintentional.[19] Moreover, I argue that psychoanalysis is a modern liberal discourse because it seeks to apply the scientific method to everyday life as it develops a practice centered on neutrality and uncensored speech. Unfortunately, not only has modern democracy itself come under attack by the Left and the Right but the analytic idea of neutrality has also been rejected by people inside and outside of psychoanalysis.[20]

One reason why the modern concept of neutrality has been criticized is that people do not accept the possibility of being unbiased and objective. Instead of seeing neutrality as a necessary but impossible ideal, many only point to its failures.[21] For example, while we want our modern legal systems to treat everyone in an equal way and judge evidence from an impartial perspective, it is clear that the system is often biased and discriminatory. In response to the evidence of this lack of neutrality, many people on the Left reject the very ideals of objectivity and impartiality, and so they end up making universal human rights impossible.[22] I counter that the only way we know a system is unjust is if we compare it to the ideals of justice, and so even the people who appear to reject modern universality are still invested in this standard. Likewise, the people who reject the value of reason and objectivity still want their arguments to be understood through reason and without bias.

As the global fight against climate change and the Covid-19 pandemic has shown, there is no way to deal with our most pressing problems if we deny modern science and refuse to think in global universal terms.[23] As difficult as the task may be, we have to fight against all of the ideologies that are preventing us from basing our public policies on reason and empirical evidence. In other words, the cultural rebellion against reason, science, and democracy has profound implications for our daily lives.[24]

It is also necessary to see that global capitalism is not the central problem in our world because inequality, prejudice, and exploitation are even more prevalent in the premodern culture. For many people on the Left, capitalism is the evil Other that is responsible for all problems, but as Marx indicated, capitalism is a driving force that overcomes all fixed premodern traditions and beliefs.[25] We thus need to find a way to regulate and control modern capitalism, but we also have to see how this system has helped to bring billions of people out of poverty for the first time in human history. Instead of the Left-wing rejection of global capitalism and the Right-wing idealization of the free market, we need to push for a form of capitalism that combines individual freedom with social responsibility on a global level.

Notes

1 Freud, Sigmund. *Psychopathology of everyday life*. Penguin Books, 1938.
2 Haidt, Jonathan. *The righteous mind: Why good people are divided by politics and religion*. Vintage, 2012.
3 Samuels, Robert. *Psychoanalyzing the politics of the new brain sciences*. Springer, 2017.
4 Klein, Ezra. *Why we're polarized*. Simon and Schuster, 2020.
5 Robin, Corey. *The reactionary mind: Conservatism from Edmund Burke to Sarah Palin*. Oxford University Press, 2011.
6 DiAngelo, Robin. *White fragility: Why it's so hard for white people to talk about racism*. Beacon Press, 2018.
7 Pagden, Anthony. *The enlightenment: and why it still matters*. Oxford University Press, 2013.
8 Samuels, Robert. "Science and the reality principle." *Freud for the Twenty-First Century*. Palgrave Pivot, 2019, 5–16.
9 Karatani, Kojin. *The structure of world history: From modes of production to modes of exchange*. Duke University Press, 2014.
10 Samuels, Robert. "(Liberal) Narcissism." *Routledge Handbook of Psychoanalytic Political Theory*. Routledge, 2019, 151–161.
11 Rifkin, Jeremy. *The age of access: The new culture of hypercapitalism*. Penguin, 2001.
12 Arnason, Johann P. "Nationalism, globalization and modernity." *Theory, Culture & Society* 7.2–3 (1990): 207–236.
13 Samuels, Robert. "Logos, global justice, and the reality principle." *Zizek and the Rhetorical Unconscious*. Palgrave Macmillan, 2020, 65–86.
14 Cole, Alyson Manda. *The cult of true victimhood: From the war on welfare to the war on terror*. Stanford University Press, 2007.
15 Campbell, Bradley, and Jason Manning. *The rise of victimhood culture: Microaggressions, safe spaces, and the new culture wars*. Springer, 2018.
16 Samuels, Robert. "Catharsis: The politics of enjoyment." *Zizek and the Rhetorical Unconscious*. Palgrave Macmillan, 2020, 7–31.
17 Kernberg, Otto. "Borderline personality organization." *Journal of the American Psychoanalytic Association* 15.3 (1967): 641–685.
18 Miller, Joshua D., Thomas A. Widiger, and W. Keith Campbell. "Narcissistic personality disorder and the DSM-V." *Journal of Abnormal Psychology* 119.4 (2010): 640.
19 Jimenez, Guillermo C. *Red genes, blue genes: Exposing political irrationality*. Autonomedia, 2009.
20 Thompson, M. Guy. "Freud's conception of neutrality." *Contemporary Psychoanalysis* 32.1 (1996): 25–42.
21 Renik, Owen. "The perils of neutrality." *The Psychoanalytic Quarterly* 65.3 (1996): 495–517.
22 Boyle, James. "The politics of reason: Critical legal theory and local social thought." *University of Pennsylvania Law Review*133.4 (1985): 685–780.

23 Pinker, Steven. *Enlightenment now: The case for reason, science, humanism, and progress*. Penguin, 2018.
24 Rensmann, Lars. *The politics of unreason: The Frankfurt School and the origins of modern antisemitism*. Suny Press, 2017.
25 Marx, Karl and Friedrich Engels. *The communist manifesto*. Penguin, 2002.

2 Jonathan Haidt and the Five Political Ideologies

In analyzing Jonathan Haidt's *The Righteous Mind: Why Good People Are Divided by Politics and Religion*, I provide a framework for understanding five dominant forms of political ideology circulating in the world today.[1] Although Haidt does articulate a way of distinguishing among a diverse set of belief systems, his lack of psychoanalytic understanding blocks him from fully comprehending the structure and cause of the ideologies he discusses. Moreover, by not including unconscious processes in his descriptions, he ends up relying on questionable assumptions derived mostly from evolutionary psychology.[2] As we shall see, a problem with this approach is that it tends to naturalize social hierarchies and remove subjectivity from political beliefs. It will therefore be my argument that by replacing the new brain sciences with psychoanalysis as an explanatory theory, we can better understand how political ideologies function in the world today.[3]

The Moral Instinct

Haidt begins his book by directly tying his theory of political ideology to an evolutionary understanding of human nature:

> I want to show you that an obsession with righteousness (leading inevitably to self-righteousness) is the normal human condition. It is a feature of our evolutionary design, not a bug or error that crept into minds that would otherwise be objective and rational.
>
> (xx)

From Haidt's perspective, political ideology is grounded in natural selection, and so biological determinism represents the key driving force behind political affiliation and our desire to be righteous.[4] Two things should strike us about this interpretative frame: the first is that it derives contemporary

DOI: 10.4324/9781003199649-2

beliefs and subjectivity from inherited mental programs, and the second is that politics is determined to be guided by the desire to be righteous. Of course, what it means to be righteous is open to debate, but for now, we can consider it to indicate the goal of people to be seen by themselves and others as being morally correct.

For Haidt, the desire to equate politics with morality relies in part on the notion that we are shaped by unconscious mental programs derived from evolution, and these intuitive reactions to the world are combined with after-the-fact moral rationalizations: "Intuitions come first, strategic reasoning second" (367). In this theory of the evolutionary unconscious, which is so popular in contemporary neuroscience, behavioral economics, and evolutionary psychology, the guiding principle is that we are not aware of why we think or do things because most of our mental processes are automatic programs derived from a universal, biological human nature.[5] Instead of affirming Freud's principle that the unconscious is developed through repression and other defense mechanisms, the guiding principle in the new brain sciences is that before we can deceive ourselves about our own thoughts, we are already defined by inherited responses that we have no control of and of which we are not aware.[6] This evolutionary theory of the unconscious, which itself represses psychoanalysis, is then coupled with the deceptive nature of our own self-consciousness: since we do not know why we do things, we have to come up with explanations after the fact to rationalize unknown evolutionary programs.[7]

One of the problems with Haidt's approach is that it relies on biological determinism, and this theory itself can be considered to be a psychopathological ideology. By eliminating the need to consider cultural and subjective factors, his universal model of human nature feeds into the libertarian backlash against social regulation and the psychoanalytic unconscious.[8] As I argue in *Psychoanalyzing Politics of the New Brain Sciences*, evolutionary psychology is often shaped by an underlying set of political beliefs, which happen to re-enforce many aspects of contemporary Right-wing politics. For instance, in saying that our human nature is universal and biological, the need for government regulation or public education is greatly reduced. After all, if we are programmed by our genes to act certain ways, then it makes no sense to think about the roles played by culture, politics, history, or language. Just as Margaret Thatcher said that there is no society, evolutionary psychology tends to be inherently anti-social and serves to justify a Right-wing, libertarian backlash against government regulation, taxes, and welfare programs.[9]

While libertarians may argue that the only thing they want is liberty, their desire to be free from social control can be seen as an unconscious political project centered on the acknowledgment and then rejection of social regulation and sacrifice. As a backlash, reactionary movement, Right-wing ideology is obsessed with what it is trying to reject.[10] For example, the current promotion of free speech is centered on seeing the Left as trying to censor the thoughts and words of people through the imposition of political correctness.[11] In this structure, the Right projects the super-ego onto the Left, and then in order to protect the freedom of its impulses (the id), it attacks the externalized super-ego and sees this defiance as a form of freedom. Of course, this dialectic is mostly unconscious because it relies on the processes of denial, splitting, projection, and projective identification.[12] These defenses are not conscious, and they do not require intentional control; rather political ideologies are psychopathological because they are founded on a lack of self-awareness. Moreover, there is no need to turn to evolutionary psychology or biology in order to understand these belief systems because they are defined by the combination of subjective defensive mechanisms and shared cultural content.

Anti-Science Science

To understand Haidt's approach, it is thus important to realize that he sees politics through his own unacknowledged Right-wing libertarian perspective. In fact, we will discover that underlying his entire project is a desire to use modern science to return to premodern conservative religion while also rejecting the value of postmodern social movements for minority rights.[13] Importantly, a driving force behind this unannounced desire to reconcile religion and science is that he seeks to reduce the tension caused by the conflict between conservative and liberal ideologies. As a way of realizing the pleasure principle's goal of avoiding all tension and conflict, he is able to rid the world of the anxiety caused by the postmodern confrontation between the modern fight for equal justice and the premodern reliance on a social hierarchy based on patriarchy, prejudice, and aristocracy. This underlying desire is partially exposed in the following passage: "When I was a teenager I wished for world peace, but now I yearn for a world in which competing ideologies are kept in balance" (xx). As a symptom of the return of his repressed awareness, Haidt indicates that his desire for peace and balance drives his politics and his understanding of political ideology. By seeking to find a happy medium between liberal and conservative worldviews, he represents his position as being centrist, but this claim to be fair and balanced hides his investment in an underlying Right-wing ideology. Although some would argue that what is missing in our political world today is moderates who can balance the extremes of the Left and the Right, psychoanalysis tells us that compromise formations often represent a hidden maintenance of what one is trying to avoid.[14] Furthermore, if one combines two wrong perspectives, and then finds their happy medium, that does not mean that one has discovered the truth. In fact, when people declare that they are not ideological, and they just want to take on a fact-based perspective, they are often simply hiding their own ideological biases, and in Haidt's case, his bias is centered on the retention of premodern religious beliefs and a lack of sensitivity towards people who have suffered political oppression. He also follows many libertarians in attacking liberals and academic thinkers even though he himself is an academic who at times identifies with being a true liberal.[15]

What is so intriguing about Haidt's work is that he unintentionally exposes different aspects of his own ideological psychopathology. For instance, in his description of moral reasoning, we gain an understanding of how opportunists like Donald Trump and other authoritarian leaders are able to manipulate others for their own gain without concern for the effect they have on others: "Keep your eye on the intuitions, and don't take people's moral arguments at face value. They're mostly post hoc constructions made up on the fly, crafted to advance one or more strategic objectives" (xxi). Since Haidt believes that we are driven by unconscious mental programs derived from natural selection, our moral reasoning can only be a social skill used to achieve our political agendas. From this perspective, morality has nothing to do with the truth since we cannot know the truth, but what we can know is our own way of rationalizing our actions after the fact. According to this logic, the reason then why we should not get upset at other people who disagree with us is that they do not really believe in the truth of their own beliefs either. Society is reduced here to the battle between isolated individuals each seeking to out-manipulate the other. Furthermore, since we should recognize that moral arguments are only "post hoc constructions," then we should not concern ourselves with the morality of anyone's acts or words.[16] In other words, Haidt's focus on moral righteousness turns out to be a false perspective since, according to his theory, moral virtue cannot be known and because it is part of a universal human nature programmed through evolution. Instead, from Haidt's perspective, political ideologies must be fictional rationalizations generated in order to justify unknown biological processes.

If we want to understand a Right-wing libertarian like Donald Trump, then, it is helpful to see what Haidt is revealing about his own pseudo-scientific theory. In a form of borderline personality splitting, sociopaths like Trump are pure opportunists who are not concerned with truth; rather, they seek to manipulate others by performing moral reasoning as a social skill.[17] One reason why, then, someone like Trump appears to show so little empathy is that his relationship with other people is primarily based on manipulation and not care or concern.[18] As a pragmatic opportunist, he only does things to further his own agenda, but we still should ask how this psychopathology relates to evolutionary psychology? An answer to this question is that if you believe that people are controlled by unknowable biological factors, then you are in the same position as someone who does not care about how their actions affect others. My argument is not that Trump and other libertarians believe we are guided by our genes; rather, my point is that you end up with the same ideology if you are an evolutionary psychologist or a sociopathic opportunist; in both cases, there is no need to think about your own motivations or to care about the feelings of other people since these inner states are unknowable, and the only thing we do know is how we can use our moral reasoning to manipulate other people through the usage of post hoc fabrications.

I have been using the terms sociopath and borderline personality to point to the same set of unconscious processes: denial, splitting, and projection.[19] For Freud, these structures were often seen as perversions since they are centered on the splitting of the mind between the super-ego (conscience) and the id (impulses).[20] While neurotics use the defense mechanism of repression to lie to themselves in order to hide their immoral intentions and guilty acts, perverts appear to be able to act on their impulses with little concern for shame or guilt. However, Freud found that many of these subjects actually split their personalities between a moral self and an immoral self, and instead of the immoral self being unconscious, the two halves of the self are compartmentalized so that the person shifts between two entirely opposed perspectives.[21] This splitting creates a structure where the self and the other are either idealized or debased, and this polarization is necessary to avoid feelings of ambiguity, ambivalence, and complexity.[22] For Freud, in an effort to escape symbolic and real incest, the person in love has to separate affection from desire, and so the ones we love, we idealize, but the ones we desire, we debase.[23] As an example of what he called the Madonna–Whore complex, men within this structure tend to see women as either pure or corrupted, and they can only have sex with the corrupted ones because the idealized pure women remind them unconsciously of their mothers. If we generalize from this theory and remove it from the classic Oedipal structure, we see that Freud was positing that the way certain people escape feelings of guilt and shame is by manipulating others whom they devalue. Thus, while Trump may love his daughter, he has virtually no problem exploiting anyone else.

In Haidt's case, this borderline splitting is represented through the following theoretical model: "The central metaphor of these four chapters is that the mind is divided, like a rider on an elephant, and the rider's job is to serve the elephant" (xxi). For Haidt, the human mind is split between the conscious rational ego and the unconscious instincts derived from biology. Although it appears that Haidt is describing the Freudian distinction between the unconscious and consciousness, his focus on seeing our evolved mental programs as unconscious results in a polarized splitting. Since the borderline personality is not centered on lying to oneself in the process of repression, what one is dealing with instead is the idea that one lies to others because one does not know oneself or care about other people. Due to the fact that the libertarian has externalized the super-ego, all that is left is amoral opportunism.

Following the Leader

Amoral opportunists, therefore, only care about the power they have over other people, but they need this power to be recognized freely by others.[24] Part of this pathology requires a lack of self-reflection and the realization that when one is powerful, one can do whatever one wants. Thus, when Trump declared that the rich and powerful can grab women wherever they desire, he was revealing the essence of perverse sociopaths: they justify their behavior through post hoc moral reasoning, but their actions are guided by the pursuit of their own pleasure, which entails suspending feelings of guilt, shame, and empathy.[25] One way to accomplish this externalization of the super-ego is to follow the evolutionary psychologist who believes that our morality is hard-wired into our unknowable brains. It is thus not our fault if we harm others since nothing can be our fault when we are driven by inherited programs.

While this theory of sociopathic libertarianism can help us to understand the leaders of this political movement, the question remains of why would people support amoral opportunists like Trump, Putin, Orban, Erdogan, and Duterte. One possible explanation is that masochists identify with the power of sadists since they can live vicariously through the freedom and enjoyment of people who act without shame or guilt.[26] Through a process of unconscious social identification, followers fantasize that they have the same power as their leaders. Trump helped to reveal this structure when he said that he could shoot someone in public, and he still would not lose his supporters. From a psychoanalytic perspective, this level of blind submission is in part the result of people trying to escape from their own freedom and responsibility by submitting to the will of powerful figures. However, for Haidt, the main explanation for political identity and identification is based on the sharing of moral rationalizations: "People bind themselves into political teams that share moral narratives. Once they accept a particular narrative, they become blind to alternative moral worlds" (xxiii). This popular theory posits that our political ideologies are enabled by our tendency to see things from the perspective of our particular social group. Similar to Marx's ideas that the ruling ideas come from the ruling class, Haidt affirms that group loyalty determines the relationship between individuals and political ideologies.[27] Yet, it is still unclear why people pick particular leaders to follow loyally. Does an individual's particular psychopathology make them susceptible to specific leaders and ideologies? Haidt does not answer this question because he has no real model of subjectivity since he can always fall back on evolutionary psychology to explain everything.

Making matters worse is that Haidt adds to the confusion by not clearly differentiating between conservatives and the Right on the one hand and liberals and the Left on the other hand. In fact, even when he does try to account for these differences, they quickly become muddled: "Readers from outside the United States may want to swap in the words progressive or left-wing whenever I say liberal" (xxiii). Since one of the aims of his book is to clarify the differences among distinct ideologies, it is confusing that he equates liberals with progressives and the Left. He also fails to see the connection between libertarians and the Right, and this lack of clarity frames his entire discourse. In fact, I will show how we should clearly distinguish the Left from liberals and the libertarian Right from conservatives, and if we do not make these distinctions, we will fall into a polarized, split discourse pitting one extreme against the other.

Against the Liberal University

In terms of Haidt's own theory, splitting often occurs between his theory of evolutionary psychology and what he calls Kohlberg's liberal cognitive psychology: "he transformed moral psychology into a boomer-friendly ode to justice, and he gave them a tool to measure children's progress toward the liberal ideal" (10). Haidt's criticism of liberalism is interesting here because he will describe himself as a formal liberal who had a conversion after a trip to India, where he began to see the value of religion. Like the narrative of a born-again Christian, Haidt relates how he turned against his former self and began to see the wrongness of the secular liberal academic culture he had once endorsed.[28] Similar to the Right-wing attack on liberal universities, Haidt will turn to religious cultures and evolutionary psychology to reject the progressive values he once supported. This conversion narrative not only allows him to privilege the hard science of biology over the soft science of cognitive psychology, but it also helps him to ignore the oppressive aspects of many traditional cultures he now valorizes.

One of the things that shapes Haidt's backlash against liberal academic culture is the fact that sees this ideology as focused on justice and not on other more conservative values: "by using a framework that predefined morality as justice while denigrating authority, hierarchy, and tradition, it was inevitable that the research would support worldviews that were secular, questioning, and egalitarian" (10). Here the true reactionary nature of his discourse is presented as he seeks to posit that modern liberalism is biased because it does not value authority, hierarchy, and tradition, and it is these conservative values that will determine how he defines competing political ideologies. Of course, on one level, Haidt is correct to say that modern liberalism does devalue the premodern conservative focus on authority, hierarchy, and tradition. Since modernity is centered on replacing religion with science, feudalism with capitalism, and monarchy with democracy, it privileges a particular worldview centered on universal human rights, empirical science, and secularism.[29] At its best, liberal academic culture represents the movement of global progress through its reliance on democratic law, egalitarian principles, and fact-based knowledge, and so it is strange that an academic like Haidt would turn on the very discourse that makes his work possible.[30] After all, he must want people to read his work by applying reason, and since he relies on the "science" of evolution to ground his theories, he must believe in the modern principles of scientific research, and yet, he sees academic discourse as the problem and not the solution. His own book thus must be read through the lens of an ironic splitting because he wants to use modern reason to argue against modern reason.

In looking at the work of different moral psychologists, Haidt finds the same privileging of liberal political ideology, which he attempts to discredit and debase: "morality is about treating individuals well. It's about harm and fairness (not loyalty, respect, duty, piety, patriotism, or tradition)" (12). From Haidt's perspective, what is so wrong with this secular, liberal academic perspective on human psychology is that it focuses on harm and fairness as core values as it tends to deny the importance of loyalty, duty, piety, patriotism, and tradition. Although, he will later argue that we need to value all of these moral traits equally, what he is doing here is concentrating on why the liberal desire for equality and the Leftist fight against harm should be balanced by a return to traditional hierarchies and loyalties. Like many other post-postmodern reactionary discourses on the Right, this call to return to traditional values is insensitive to the suffering that these premodern hierarchies have caused different minority groups, and it also fails to clearly differentiate the modern liberal quest for equality and the postmodern fight for minority rights.[31]

The Tolerance of Intolerance

At times, his criticism of secular liberalism sounds like a Christian fundamentalist call to return to strict authority and the respect for traditional values: "Schools and families should therefore embody progressive principles of equality and autonomy (not authoritarian principles that enable elders to train and constrain children)" (12). In his call for elders to train and constrain children, he appears to be going against his own belief that morality is hard-wired into our brains, but this return to "family values" reveals a high tolerance for conservative oppression by libertarians who like to present themselves as being unbiased and middle-ground rationalists. In reality, what we often find in libertarian discourse is an insensitivity towards people who have suffered from premodern conservative social hierarchies sustained by religion and patriarchy. This lack of empathy for the suffering of others is rationalized by Haidt in seeing this concern as just one moral value that has to be balanced with other values, like loyalty, tradition, and authority.

At the foundation of Right-wing libertarian ideology, we find four interacting components: a lack of empathy for the suffering of disempowered groups, a tolerance of intolerant conservative practices, a rejection of modern liberalism, and an externalization of the super-ego. Haidt's discourse unintentionally supports these four components by hiding under the banner of being fair and balanced, which is also the "ironic" tagline of the Right-wing Fox News.[32] In Haidt's case, he seeks to transcend political polarization by affirming a mythical middle-ground, but his own rhetoric reveals a very different agenda.

The Modern Liberal Dialectic

Another related aspect of Haidt's criticism of liberalism is that at times, he focuses on equality, and other times, he sees individualism as the main concern. Although universal equality and individualism are theoretical opposites, it is true that a central dialectic of modernity is the protection of both universal rights and individual freedom; one way that modern liberalism is able to combine these opposite values is through the separation of the private and the public realms; for instance, modern democratic law implies that you are free in private, but in public, you must submit to universal laws and norms.[33] Haidt fudges his argument by sometimes relating liberalism to pure individualism, and other times, he equates liberalism with the sole value of equal justice (17). In fact, the type of individualism referenced by Haidt should be equated with libertarianism since it is centered on the needs of the isolated individual. In contrast, modern liberalism places individual freedom in relation to social restrictions and protected rights. It is also reductive to reduce the choices societies make to two possibilities: either one focuses on the group or one focuses on the individual. In Haidt's simplistic, binary historical account, premodernity is equated with society and modernity with the individual: "The sociocentric answer dominated most of the ancient world, but the individualistic answer became a powerful rival during the Enlightenment" (17). One problem with this reading of history is that it represses how modern liberalism was centered on the three social institutions of science, democracy, and capitalism, and while these social organizations helped to free people from premodern hierarchies and religious beliefs, they did not result in a pure promotion of the individual over society. After all, science, democracy, and capitalism are shared social systems requiring the submission of isolated individuals to universalizing processes.[34] Not only, then does Haidt obscure what modernity means, but he also idealizes premodernity by seeing it as focused on social values. Instead of addressing the role played by prejudice, discrimination, and exploitation in premodern cultures, he wants to emphasize the more ideal aspects of traditional hierarchies.

By playing fast and loose with his terminology and history, Haidt reveals the way our views of ourselves and the world are shaped by the concepts we use to frame our perceptions. This focus on the power of ideas to frame how reality is viewed is often called social construction theory because this postmodern philosophy stresses how our perceptions of reality are not natural and neutral since they are determined by cultural and historical lenses.[35] However, for strategic reasons, Haidt does not want to focus on the constructed nature of discourse because he desires to return to a biological model of the mind as he discredits the humanities and other social sciences. At the same time, then, he has to rely on science to makes his evolutionary theories appear credible and correct, he also seeks to discredit modern science itself. This contradictory discourse is made possible in part by his repression of the rhetorical foundations of his analysis. Since libertarians want to be able to say whatever they want without concern for how they are affecting other groups, they have to deny the importance of words, and this often entails railing against postmodern theory, political correctness, social constructivism, and identity politics.[36]

Against Modern Reason

Haidt's anti-Left and anti-liberal biases are evident in the following that claims European countries with strong social welfare programs are not sociocentric because their focus is on protecting the individual (17). Since he wants to equate liberalism with individualism and conservatism with social welfare, he is forced to make the absurd claim that advanced welfare programs are the product of individualism and not socialism. Moreover, what he refuses to accept is the role played by Leftist social movements in the expansion of social welfare programs and democratic justice. Therefore, due to his need to demonize the Left and critique liberals, he ends up rewriting history and misrepresenting contemporary political ideologies.

A common move that we often see in the brain sciences is to use reason to critique reason.[37] Often the goal of this strategy is to show how the promotion of reason over emotion in Western philosophy and culture is just a way of making us think that we are more in control of our minds than we really are. In fact, he calls the Western privileging of reason over the passions the rationalist delusion (34). While Freud argued that the main way to overcome our tendency to be deluded is to learn how to be unbiased through the empirical utilization of reason in the form of reality testing, Haidt wants to reverse this process by claiming that our investment in reason is itself a delusion.[38] Moreover, instead of seeing reason as the path beyond religious thinking and other illusions and superstitions, he equates modern reason with the role of the sacred in a cult. Of course, Haidt expects his readers to interpret his words in a reasonable way, and he expects to be treated in a reasonable fashion as he argues by using reason, but still he wants to demonize reason and equate it with a religious delusion.

It is very telling that in the age of fake news, alternative facts, and conspiracy theories, we would find an academic writer devaluing reason and promoting emotions and intuitions as the true source of moral understanding.[39] This criticism of liberal reason is coupled with a dismissal of what he sees as the Left-wing postmodern social sciences (36). Since evolutionary psychologists are often being rightly accused of social Darwinism, they must constantly defend themselves by attacking competing discourses and by denying the implications of their own work.[40] Like Steven Pinker, Haidt tends to dismiss the social sciences as a form of moral relativism that does not understand biology and which incorrectly argues that we are defined by nurture through a process of socialization.[41]

Haidt manages to accuse postmodern scientists of being unconcerned with morality while being moral relativists and strict moralists at the same time:

> The second wave of moralism was the radical politics that washed over universities in America, Europe, and Latin America in the 1960s and 1970s. Radical reformers usually want to believe that human nature is a blank slate on which any utopian vision can be sketched. (37)

Following the Right-wing attack on "liberal universities," Haidt insists that these institutions have been taken over by radical Left-wing political activists who want to deny biology and evolution in order to provide the false hope that social hierarchies can be resisted and transformed.[42] This common backlash against the academic Left is often generated through the selection of extreme examples that are then exaggerated and taken out of context.[43] Of course, it is very ironic that Haidt attacks teachers for not basing their analysis on truth and reason when he has just spent several pages critiquing the use of reason. Although it should be clear that some Left-wing thinkers and activists do deny any natural forces shaping human life, many see a dialectic between nature and nurture.

Another rhetorical move that Haidt shares with other Right-wing thinkers and politicians is his claim that scientists like him are now the real victims of society because they constantly have their free speech censored by the radical Left: "Wilson therefore deserves to be called a prophet of moral psychology. He was harassed and excoriated in print and in public" (38).

This reference to E.O. Wilson is based on the idea that people do not want to hear the connections among gender and genes or race and IQ scores, and so they attack the scientists, who are just trying to state scientific facts. As we shall see, Haidt himself says many provocative and questionable things, but he still positions himself as an innocent victim when he is criticized for some of his ideas.[44] Since the libertarian Right sees their free speech as an ultimate value, they do not think they should have to worry about offending other people. On one level, it is true that science should be able to follow truth wherever it goes, but when people are using pseudoscience to make oppressive statements, then they are no longer engaged in unbiased science, and instead, they are simply presenting prejudices, stereotypes, and hate speech under the cover of pure science. Therefore, as the academic Left attempts to stop the circulation of oppressive premodern conservative ideology, the reactionary Right pretends that it is just stating the facts when it is often really rejecting liberal reason and recirculating premodern prejudices.

Nature over Nurture

Haidt's contradictory relation to science and reason is evident in his use of evolutionary science, whose development he describes as presenting, "an alternative approach to morality, one whose foundation was the emotions, and the emotions were assumed to have been shaped by evolution" (41). There are two different moves that Haidt makes at this point in his text: the first is to privilege emotion over reason, and the second is to center human emotion on evolution. Importantly, these two steps lead to a model of biological determinism, and yet he often wants to claim that he is not expressing this theory because he also at times takes culture into account.[45]

In order to define our current political ideologies, Haidt focuses on core moral values, and he posits that these values are intuitive social judgments and not the result of culture, language, education, or individual experience. One way that he tries to prove this view is by showing how even infants make social and moral judgments: "But when psychologists dug deeper, they found that infants come equipped with innate abilities to understand their social world as well" (74). Although it is extremely difficult to interpret what is going on in an infant's mind, Haidt believes that experiments prove that our ability to make moral judgments must be hard-wired into our brain through evolution. Of course, the reality may be that the experimenters are simply projecting their own understandings of social norms onto these infants, and so the tests say more about the testers than the subjects under study.[46]

If we accept this notion that our morals are derived from or biological instincts, and we also agree that political beliefs are defined by these moral traits, then we must conclude that our political ideologies are inherited through natural selection. People are thus born to be liberals, conservatives, or libertarians, and at times, Haidt does appear to be making arguments based purely on biological determinism, but at other times, he allows for different factors to influence our inherited intuitions. In using his model of the emotional elephant being steered by the rational rider, he indicates that our intuitive moral judgments can be influenced by our reasoning self: "But if there is affection, admiration, or a desire to please the other person, then the elephant leans toward that person and the rider tries to find the truth in the other person's arguments" (80). In positing that our emotions (elephants) can be steered by other people's emotions, he indicates that it is not so much our rational self that influences our emotion-based intuitions; instead, other people's emotional intuitions can steer our own emotional intuitions. The subtle move here is to base politics and political influence on inherited mental programs; even when we do overcome our initial moral biases, the change occurs on a purely non-conscious intuitive level. In this structure, reason and culture are bypassed at both ends.

If, as Haidt insists, our moral emotions are derived from instinctual mental programs, and even when we are influenced by others, this social communication occurs on the level of intuitive emotions, then Haidt's own book should be an example of this evolutionary model. In fact, he does argue that he did take this approach in the construction of his work:

> I threw in historical anecdotes, quotations from the ancients, and praise of a few visionaries. I set up metaphors (such as the rider and the elephant) that will recur throughout the book. I did these things in order to "tune up" your intuitions about moral psychology.
>
> (59)

Haidt's argument here is that his use of metaphors, stories, quotations, and praise by others allowed him the ability to access our intuitions by communicating his own intuitive emotions. The irony here is that he wants to posit that all of these language-based rhetorical strategies are actually emotional intuitions determined by biological mental programs. However, it should be clear that stories and metaphors are not biological because they define culture and the very thing that separate us from other animals.[47]

What Makes Us Human

For Freud, what makes us human is that we are not driven purely by instincts or evolution; instead, anything can be a source of pleasure, and we often act in self-destructive ways.[48] Moreover, the ability of our minds to transcend material reality through thought indicates that our free will comes in part by our double transcendence of both nature and reality. Likewise, since we are linguistic beings, our words and symbols can have multiple meanings and can serve the purpose of hiding our true intentions and displacing our emotions through symbolic substitution. Finally, our ability to reason enables us to go beyond our drive to pursue only our own pleasure. In fact, Freud defines pleasure as the release of mental tension, and this theory of the pleasure principle means that our emotions are not centered on survival or reproduction.[49]

From a psychoanalytic perspective, it thus makes no sense to say that our emotions and intuitions are purely instinctual or that they can be studied by experimenting on non-human animals or infants. For human beings, the existence of free will, consciousness, unconscious processes, and shared reason entails a radical break with nature, evolution, and instinct. One reason why, then, it is contradictory for Haidt to say that he turned to metaphors and stories to prove the guiding force of instinctual intuitions is that stories and metaphors are human symbolic constructions transcending our natural impulses and empirical reality. However, in his libertarian quest to deny the importance of culture and language, he simply denies the content of his own discourse.

It is important to stress that this turn to a biological model of the human mind is represented in terms of a political culture war: "the political climate was harsh for people such as Wilson who dared to suggest that evolutionary thinking was a valid way to examine human behavior" (78). One reason why people respond to evolutionary psychology in such a negative way is that it undermines the notion that we can overcome inherited social structures through the collective use of reason. Since biological determinism tends to naturalize social hierarchies, it is seen as a conservative ideology justifying the dominance of men over women and the powerful over the disempowered.[50] Instead of seeing that power structures are produced and maintained by people through the use of language, laws, punishment, and other social mechanisms, evolutionary psychology wants to see social hierarchies as natural and inevitable, and this is one reason why they like to refer to primates as an example of social organization.

Naturalizing Conservative Ideology

By refusing to acknowledge the difference between humans and other animals, biological theories of the mind often end up reinforcing conservative ideologies. For example, in the following example, we see how conservative views of gender differences can be derived from the study of primates:

> mammals face the challenge of caring for and nurturing their children for a long time … And human babies, whose brains are so enormous that a child must be pushed out through the birth canal a year before he or she can walk, are bets so huge that a woman can't even put her chips on the table by herself.
>
> (153)

Since primate mothers need help delivering and caring for their children, the traits and preferences of women are said to be shaped by this biological imperative. Here nature is used to justify gender differences, which are then used to help structure a conservative social order where men are free to spread their seed, while women have to stay at home and tend to their breed.[51]

The evolutionary need for mothers to tend to their babies is extended to explain why women are more caring and empathic:

> Given the number of people who pool their resources to bet on each child, evolution favored women and (to a lesser extent) men who had an automatic reaction to signs of need or suffering, such as crying, from children in their midst (who, in ancient times, were likely to be kin).
>
> (153)

Just as Aristotle posited that men should dominate women because reason is superior to emotion, evolutionary psychologists argue that the concern for others is primarily a female attribute, and so political ideologies based on care must be seen as female-centered belief systems.[52] From this reductive perspective, it is implied that conservatives are masculine because they focus on authority and hierarchy, while liberals are female because they emphasize and have an ethic of care.

Perhaps Haidt would say that my criticism of his biological determinism is unfair because he does open up a space for other influences. In fact, the following passage does appear to limit the scope of evolutionary psychology:

> De Waal did not claim that chimpanzees had morality; he argued only that chimps (and other apes) have most of the psychological building blocks that humans use to construct moral systems and communities. These building blocks are largely emotional, such as feelings of sympathy, fear, anger, and affection.
>
> (39)

This is a tricky passage because it begins by arguing that other animals have the same moral building blocks, and so these programs can be open to human content and change, and yet by also stating that these animals have the same feelings of anger, sympathy, and fear, human emotions are once again reduced to instinctual mental programs.[53]

A key aspect of conservative ideology has always been the process of claiming that social hierarchies are the result of natural or divine order, and so there is no reason to resist them or call them into question.[54] Theocratic ideologies rely on this process of naturalizing culture because they need to make oppression seem inevitable and fated by the will of a higher power. Moreover, the paradox of these premodern conservative ideologies is that even the people in power have to submit to an already established social order. In fact, the essence of conservativism is to *conserve* the social system and the current distribution of power, which is seen as being a product of faith, fate, and belief. The moral attributes of loyalty, authority, and sanctity that Haidt wants to valorize therefore belong to a conservative ideology centered on the need to have people submit to a system that controls and oppresses them. We shall see in later chapters that this emphasis on submission to authority points to a masochistic foundation of conservative subjectivity.

Haidt's Five Traits of Ideology

When Haidt finally gets to his theory of the five moral political ideologies, we see that he relates conservative values to three of the moral attributes driving these belief systems: "The five rows illustrate violations of Care (hurting a child), Fairness (profiting from someone else's undeserved loss), Loyalty (criticizing your nation to outsiders), Authority (disrespecting your father), and Sanctity (acting in a degrading or disgusting way)" (152). By structuring his analysis in this way, he stacks the deck against liberalism since he wants to argue that the more moral traits a political order supports, the better it must be. In other words, he sees liberals as only concerned about care and fairness, but conservatives utilize all of these moral emotions in their ideology.

The first problem, then, with Haidt's model is that it is shaped to make conservatives look good and liberals look bad because it has selected categories that cater to conservative ideology. Moreover, the connection between the traits and the political ideologies is highly questionable. For instance, in his discussion of the Left, he ties this ideology to fairness and not to the effort to protect against harm:

> On the left, concerns about equality and social justice are based in part on the Fairness foundation—wealthy and powerful groups are accused of gaining by exploiting those at the bottom while not paying their "fair share" of the tax burden.
>
> (159)

The confusion here is that the fight for equality belongs to modern liberalism and the democratic law, while the Leftist criticism of unfairness often derives from groups that have been excluded from modern equality.[55] While liberals need the Left so that more groups can be included in universal human rights, modern liberals often reject the postmodern radical revolutions of the Left, and so it is important to separate liberalism from the Left just as one needs to distinguish premodern conservatives from post-postmodern libertarians.

One reason why I have been adding historical markers to these political ideologies is that it is vital to see how each system reacts to a previous system: thus modern liberal democracy and science counter premodern conservative religion and monarchy, while the social movements on the postmodern Left reject both premodern social hierarchies and modern claims of equality, and finally, the post-postmodern libertarian Right is primarily a backlash against the postmodern Left.[56] However, it is also important to realize that the older political ideologies are never fully surpassed, and so they continue to circulate after their period of dominance has ended. Since the concepts we use to make our arguments and experiments are essential, it is important to be aware of the constructed nature of any analysis. Unfortunately, Haidt wants to downplay the roles that language and culture play in our mental and social lives, and so he is unable to fully grasp the ways his model manipulates how he perceives reality.

While it makes sense to attach authority, sanctity, and loyalty to premodern conservatives, he himself calls into question the identification of fairness with the Left: "On the left, fairness often implies equality, but on the right it means proportionality—people should be rewarded in proportion to what they contribute, even if that guarantees unequal outcomes" (160). This passage is so confusing because liberalism is often associated with the notion of equal opportunity and not equal outcomes, while the Left often fights against unequal outcomes. Moreover, the Right rarely makes claims based on fairness since they are usually concerned for the rights of isolated, competing individuals.[57] Instead of Haidt using the scientific method to clarify the reality of our political ideologies, it appears that he is unknowingly and unintentionally making an argument for the value of conservativism and the Right over liberals and the Left. Furthermore, since he does not clearly distinguish the differences among these distinct ideologies, he is able to make misleading claims.

One of the greatest areas of distortion in his discourse is his reliance on the conservative patriarchal ideology that he desires to represent as being natural and inevitable: "The male mind appears to be innately tribal—that is, structured in advance of experience so that boys and men enjoy doing the sorts of things that lead to group cohesion and success in conflicts between groups (including warfare)" (162). It is gender-based arguments like this that cause the Left to protest against evolutionary psychology.[58] In insisting that boys are more loyal and tribal, he is explaining male dominance through natural selection and not social, historical, and cultural factors. Moreover, since he privileges loyalty and authority as two key moral ingredients, he is valorizing the way patriarchy has oppressed half of humankind.[59] Of course, he would say that he is just doing science and stating the facts, but it should be clear that his science is structured by a set of reductive concepts and retroactive rationalizations.

What Haidt does not appear to grasp is the way that modern liberal science and democracy rest on universal principles constructed by humans that are not a result of natural selection.[60] We see his blindness in regard to universality, equality, democratic law, and reason in the following passage: "Kant, like Plato, wanted to discover the timeless, changeless form of the Good. He believed that morality had to be the same for all rational creatures, regardless of their cultural or individual proclivities" (139).

What is correct about this explanation of modern liberal law is that it is based on the social acceptance of abstract rules; however, these universal laws are dynamic and change throughout history as universal human rights continue to cover different groups previously excluded. In fact, one reason why it is hard to directly observe these abstract rules is that they transcend the consciousness of the isolated individual, and this is one of their main benefits: while we may not actually sign the social contract, as members of society, we cannot be ignorant of its rules, which should apply to everyone in an equal manner.[61] When these systems do fail to deliver equal treatment, it is essential for people to organize to fight for more equality: here we see how the social movements on the Left help to expand and correct liberal law and democratic principles. Social laws, then, have to be a priori because they need to pre-exist the individual observer since they are social practices transcending isolated individuals.

I have been arguing that it is essential to clearly distinguish the ideological foundations of four main ideologies: conservative, liberal, Left, and Right. Instead of seeing each of these political belief systems as being structured by instinctual mental programs, I have turned to psychoanalysis to show why we must consider the way humans break with evolution, nature, reality, and their own consciousness. Thus, if we want to understand how political ideologies function today, we need to see them as psychopathological structures that have a cultural, historical, and subjective foundation. In the next chapter, this argument is extended by looking at the question of why our politics and culture seem to be so polarized today.

Notes

1 Haidt, Jonathan. *The righteous mind: Why good people are divided by politics and religion*. Vintage, 2012.
2 Rose, Steven, Richard Charles Lewontin, and Leon Kamin. "Not in our genes: Biology, ideology and human nature." *The Wilson Quarterly* 152 (1984): 115
3 Samuels, Robert. *Psychoanalyzing the politics of the new brain sciences*. Springer, 2017.
4 Jimenez, Guillermo C. *Red genes, blue genes: Exposing political irrationality*. Autonomedia, 2009.
5 Barrett, Louise, Robin Dunbar, and John Lycett. *Human evolutionary psychology*. Princeton University Press, 2002.
6 Reber, Arthur S. "The cognitive unconscious: An evolutionary perspective." *Consciousness and Cognition* 1.2 (1992): 93–133.
7 Gilboa, Asaf, and Morris Moscovitch. "The cognitive neuroscience of confabulation: A review and a model." *Handbook of Memory Disorders* 2 (2002): 315–342.

8 Rose, Hilary, and Steven Rose. *Alas poor Darwin: Arguments against evolutionary psychology*. Random House, 2010.
9 Petersen, Michael Bang, et al. "Who deserves help? Evolutionary psychology, social emotions, and public opinion about welfare." *Political Psychology* 33.3 (2012): 395–418.
10 Norris, Pippa, and Ronald Inglehart. *Cultural backlash: Trump, Brexit, and authoritarian populism*. Cambridge University Press, 2019.
11 Hughes, Geoffrey. *Political correctness: A history of semantics and culture*. Vol. 24. John Wiley & Sons, 2011.
12 Shoesmith, Sharon. *Learning from Baby P: The politics of blame, fear and denial*. Jessica Kingsley Publishers, 2016.
13 Samuels, Robert. *Zizek and the rhetorical unconscious*. Palgrave Macmillan, 2020, 7–31.
14 Sandel, Michael J. *The tyranny of merit: What's become of the common good?* Allen Lane, 2020.
15 Horowitz, David. *Reforming our universities: The campaign for an academic bill of rights*. Regnery Publishing, 2010.
16 Strandberg, Thomas, et al. "False beliefs and confabulation can lead to lasting changes in political attitudes." *Journal of Experimental Psychology: General* 147.9 (2018): 1382.
17 Paris, Joel. "Antisocial and borderline personality disorders: Two separate diagnoses or two aspects of the same psychopathology?" *Comprehensive Psychiatry* 38.4 (1997): 237–242.
18 Adam, Emily L. *The psychopath next door: How similar are they to those behind bars? Criminality, executive functioning, and emotion processing in noncriminal psychopathy*. Diss. Queensland University of Technology, 2017.
19 Zanarini, Mary C., Jolie L. Weingeroff, and Frances R. Frankenburg. "Defense mechanisms associated with borderline personality disorder." *Journal of Personality Disorders* 23.2 (2009): 113–121.
20 Gillespie, W. Hewitt. "The general theory of sexual perversion." *International Journal of Psycho-Analysis* 37 (1956): 396–403.
21 Freud, Sigmund. "A special type of choice of object made by men (Contributions to the psychology of love I)." *The standard edition of the complete psychological works of Sigmund Freud, volume XI (1910): Five lectures on psychoanalysis, Leonardo da Vinci and other works*, trans. James Strachey and Anna Freud (London: Hogarth Press, 1957):163–176.
22 Kernberg, Otto. "The treatment of patients with borderline personality organization." *International Journal of Psycho-Analysis* 49 (1968): 600–619.
23 Hartmann, Uwe. "Sigmund Freud and his impact on our understanding of male sexual dysfunction." *The Journal of Sexual Medicine* 6.8 (2009): 2332–2339.
24 Lucas, Peter. *Ethics and Self-Knowledge*. Springer, 2011, 143–165.
25 Meloy, J. Reid. "The "polymorphously perverse" psychopath: Understanding a strong empirical relationship." *Bulletin of the Menninger Clinic* 66.3 (2002): 273–289.
26 Stekel, Wilhelm. *Sadism and Masochism-The Psychology of Hatred and Cruelty*. Vol. 2. Read Books Ltd, 2013.

27 Chua, Amy. *Political tribes: Group instinct and the fate of nations*. Penguin Books, 2019.
28 Winchester, Daniel. "Converting to continuity: Temporality and self in eastern orthodox conversion narratives." *Journal for the Scientific Study of Religion* 54.3 (2015): 439–460.
29 Pagden, Anthony. *The Enlightenment: and why it still matters*. Oxford University Press, 2013.
30 Samuels, Robert. *Teaching Writing, Rhetoric, and Reason at the Globalizing University*. Routledge, 2020.
31 Kymlicka, Will. *Multicultural citizenship: A liberal theory of minority rights*. Clarendon Press, 1995.
32 Budak, Ceren, Sharad Goel, and Justin M. Rao. "Fair and balanced? quantifying media bias through crowdsourced content analysis." *Public Opinion Quarterly* 80.S1 (2016): 250–271.
33 Wagner, Peter. *A sociology of modernity: Liberty and discipline*. Routledge, 2002.
34 Henrich, Joseph. *The WEIRDest people in the world: How the West became psychologically peculiar and particularly prosperous*. Farrar, Straus and Giroux, 2020.
35 Gergen, Kenneth J. *Social construction in context*. Sage, 2001.
36 Samuels, Robert. "The Automodern University: The Universal Individual and the Backlash against Social Discourse." *New Media, Cultural Studies, and Critical Theory after Postmodernism*. Palgrave Macmillan, New York, 2009. 105–121.
37 Samuels, Robert. "Damasio's Error: The Politics of Biological Determinism After Freud." *Psychoanalyzing the Politics of the New Brain Sciences*. Palgrave Pivot, Cham, 2017. 9–33.
38 Freud, Sigmund. *Totem and taboo: Resemblances between the psychic lives of savages and neurotics*. Good Press, 2019.
39 Emanuelson, Eric. "Fake left, fake right: Promoting an informed public in the era of alternative facts." *Administrative Law Review* 70.1 (2017): 209–232.
40 Laland, Kevin N., Gillian Brown, and Gillian R. Brown. *Sense and nonsense: Evolutionary perspectives on human behaviour*. Oxford University Press, 2011.
41 Pinker, Steven. *The blank slate: The modern denial of human nature*. Penguin, 2003.
42 Samuels, Robert. "The Backlash Politics of Evolutionary Psychology: Steven Pinker's Blank Slate." *Psychoanalyzing the Politics of the New Brain Sciences*. Palgrave Pivot, Cham, 2017. 35–58.
43 Wilson, John K. *The myth of political correctness: The conservative attack on higher education*. Duke University Press, 1995.
44 Wodak, Ruth. *The politics of fear: What right-wing populist discourses mean*. Sage, 2015.
45 Greene, Sheila. "V. Biological determinism: persisting problems for the psychology of women." *Feminism & Psychology* 14.3 (2004): 431–435.
46 Lacan, Jacques. *The four fundamental concepts of psycho-analysis*. Vol. 11. WW Norton & Company, 1998.

47 Semino, Elena. *Metaphor in discourse*. Cambridge: Cambridge University Press, 2008.
48 Freud, Sigmund. *Three essays on the theory of sexuality: The 1905 edition*. Verso Books, 2017.
49 Freud, Sigmund. "The pleasure principle." *The standard edition of the complete psychological works of Sigmund Freud* (1920).
50 Ruti, Mari. *The age of scientific sexism: How evolutionary psychology promotes gender profiling and fans the battle of the sexes*. Bloomsbury Publishing USA, 2015.
51 Eisler, Riane, and Daniel S. Levine. "Nurture, nature, and caring: We are not prisoners of our genes." *Brain and mind* 3.1 (2002): 9–52.
52 Sahlins, Marshall David. *The use and abuse of biology: An anthropological critique of sociobiology*. University of Michigan Press, 1976.
53 Haselton, Martie G., and Timothy Ketelaar. "Irrational emotions or emotional wisdom? The evolutionary psychology of affect and social behavior." *Affect in social thinking and behavior* 8 (2006): 21.
54 Huntington, Samuel P. "Conservatism as an Ideology." *The American political science review* 51.2 (1957): 454–473.
55 Bernstein, Richard J. "Rorty's liberal utopia." *Social Research* (1990): 31–72.
56 Samuels, Robert. "After Frederic Jameson: A Practical Critique of Pure Theory and Postmodernity." *New Media, Cultural Studies, and Critical Theory after Postmodernism*. Palgrave Macmillan, New York, 2009. 51–68.
57 White, Mark. *The manipulation of choice: Ethics and libertarian paternalism*. Springer, 2013.
58 Rose, Steven, Richard Charles Lewontin, and L. Kamin. "Not in our genes: Biology, ideology and human nature." *The Wilson Quarterly* 152 (1984).
59 Crane-Seeber, Jesse, and Betsy Crane. "Contesting essentialist theories of patriarchal relations: Evolutionary psychology and the denial of history." *The Journal of Men's Studies* 18.3 (2010): 218–237.
60 Moyn, Samuel. *The last utopia: human rights in history*. Harvard University Press, 2012.
61 Samuels, Robert. "Logos, Global Justice, and the Reality Principle." *Zizek and the Rhetorical Unconscious*. Palgrave Macmillan, Cham, 2020. 65–86.

3 On the Psychopathology of Polarization

In looking at Ezra Klein's *Why We're Polarized*, I endeavor to expose how the social sciences and the mass media often help to cause the phenomenon they are studying. With the case of political and social polarization, we will see that the complexity of our social lives and political ideologies can be obscured through reductive binary thinking. As a form of unconscious splitting, polarization represents a type of psychopathology.[1] In other words, our desire to see the world in terms of extreme opposites is derived from an unconscious need to avoid complexity, ambiguity, ambivalence, and ultimately reality itself. In Klein's case, he shifts between seeing politics as structured by the opposition of the Left and the Right to the opposition of liberals and conservatives and ultimately to the distinction between Democrats and Republicans. A core problem of his analysis, then, is that in its obsession to see polarization, different oppositions are utilized through unconscious processes of substitution and displacement. Moreover, the issues that I trace in his discourse have implications for how our society itself thinks about political ideologies.

Klein begins his discussion of political polarization by stressing the ways we are stuck in our ideological bubbles and how hard it is for us to consider taking a different stance or supporting a different candidate that is not pre-determined by our ideological bias:

> We are so locked into our political identities that there is virtually no candidate, no information, no condition, that can force us to change our minds. We will justify almost anything or anyone so long as it helps our side, and the result is a politics devoid of guardrails, standards, persuasion, or accountability.
>
> (xiv)

While we saw in the last chapter that Haidt traces our ideological commitments to our reliance on emotions and moral intuitions derived from

DOI: 10.4324/9781003199649-3

inherited mental programs, Klein centers his analysis primarily on social science research and his own personal observations and not on evolutionary psychology. As a journalist who runs his own media company, we shall see that his post-postmodern discourse is shaped by the contemporary blending of science, capitalism, and entertainment.[2] While in the modern period, there was a great effort to separate different realms, like the Church and the state, and democracy and capitalism, in our current period, it is often hard to see where the scientific search for empirical evidence begins and the desire to make money through entertainment ends. Furthermore, the need for content creators to generate profits by gaining an audience can push them to cater to the desire for pleasure, which Freud equated with an escape from tension and reality.[3] In other words, our entertainment culture is driven by a need to reduce conflict and deny reality, and so we should ask how is Klein's own discourse shaped by this imperative?

Instead of blaming nature or evolution for our political polarization, Klein wants to focus on how the political system itself corrupts individuals: "What is rational and even moral for us to do individually becomes destructive when done collectively" (xv). According to this logic, large social forces can get us to turn on each other by taking advantage of our own morals and values. What is productive about Klein's approach here is that it attempts to articulate the relation between individual psychology and political ideologies; since individuals acting in their own best interests can contribute to the harm of our shared social world, it is necessary to recognize the fundamental conflict and relation between society and the individual. However, although psychoanalysis is also centered on examining this basic conflict, we shall see that its approach to political ideology is much different.

For Klein, social structures have the ability to transcend the interests and knowledge of individuals, and so it is necessary to start with a systemic approach:

> We collapse systemic problems into personalized narratives, and when we do, we cloud our understanding of American politics and confuse our theories of repair. We try to fix the system by changing the people who run it, only to find that they become part of the system, too.
>
> (xvi)

While I agree that it is important not to emphasize personal stories when one is dealing with politics, the risk with this perspective is that it can completely erase the role played by individual responsibility in the formation and support of political ideologies. What we need, then, is a theoretical approach that recognizes the power of systemic structures as it also affirms the contribution of individual subjectivity.[4] Although our political ideologies transcend individual desires and thoughts, they are sustained through individual psychopathologies.[5]

In reflecting on his own writing, Klein highlights that he wants to describe a system rather than tell a story: "What I seek isn't a story but a blueprint, a map to the machine that shapes political decisions" (xviii). In seeing politics as a machine, Klein reveals that he thinks social structures are essential, and the personal narratives shaped by and shaping those structures are less important, and yet, he does seek to entertain by telling stories and providing his audience with access to personalities and personal reflections. I interpret this contradiction as symptomatic of the contemporary conflict between media entertainment and the communication of objective knowledge: Klein wants to take a scientific approach, but he also wants to sell books, and so he cannot simply describe systems from a detached, neutral perspective.[6] Caught between entertainment and science, his discourse obscures as much as it enlightens, and this combination of insight and blindness reflects the very problem he wants to explain.

Beyond Reason

An interesting effect of Klein's focus on the political system over individuals is that he tends to remove individuals from any responsibility for contemporary problems. For example, he argues that the American political system is full of rational actors, but the system itself is irrational: "We are a collection of functional parts whose efforts combine into a dysfunctional whole" (xvii). First of all, it is hard to see that everyone is acting in a rational way, and second of all, by blaming the system, you absolve people of any guilt or shame, which is one of the central goals of the pleasure principle.[7] According to psychoanalysis, people often are irrational, and they engage in self-defeating behavior whether they know it or not. In fact, one reason why individuals can be so irrational is that in their desperate attempt to escape any sense of responsibility, which would lead to feelings of guilt or shame, they blame other people and the system itself for their problems.[8] Klein participates in this psychopathological structure by removing individual responsibility from his analysis, which in turn, satisfies an audience's hunger to hear that nothing is their fault. After all, we are only victims of a corrupt system, and the victims are always innocent. Furthermore, you cannot criticize a victim, and the vengeance of the victim is always justified.[9]

The type of victim psychopathology I am describing here is based on the psychoanalytic idea that some people imagine their victimized status in order to manipulate other people on an unconscious, emotional level.[10] The goal here is not to deny that people really are victimized and abused; rather, psychoanalysis focuses on imaginary fantasies of victimhood that often displace our focus on the true victims. For example, when wealthy people on the Right claim that they have been victims of taxes, government regulations, and political correctness, they are not only trying to manipulate others by taking on a victim identity, but they are also denying the suffering of people who have really been victimized on a personal and political level.[11] While the Left tends to organize around real acts of victimization, the Right often relies on an imagined victim identity. In Klein's case, he generalizes harm to such an extent that the difference between real and imaginary victimization is often lost.

One way that his discourse feeds into this victim-based politics is through his claim that the system is so evil that the only way to achieve success in it is to be a horrible person who knows how to work it for one's advantage:

> That the worst actors are so often draped in success doesn't prove the system is broken; it proves that they understand the ways in which it truly works. That is knowledge the rest of us need, if we are to change it.
>
> (xviii)

As a mode of cynical conformity, the idea here is that the people who succeed in the corrupt system are the ones who know it is corrupt. Thus, pure amoral opportunists like Donald Trump can be successful because they do not believe in the system they are manipulating.[12] Since they know the political structure is corrupt, they do not have to worry about how their actions affect other people as they escape all responsibility for their acts.

Neo-Liberal Centrism

Although Klein self-identifies as a liberal, he claims that the system has shaped his politics to such an extent that he is no longer acting on his own beliefs: "I am motivated in part by the radicalizing realization that I am often carrying out the biddings of a system I dislike" (xviii). In this confessional discourse, Klein admits that his politics and work may just be a reflection of current American life. Instead of affirming the modern liberal beliefs in the necessary but impossible ideals of universality, objectivity, and neutrality, Klein reveals how Neo-Liberal centrists represent a fifth ideology beyond premodern conservatives, modern liberals, postmodern Leftists, and the libertarian Right. This psychopathology is centered on cynical conformity and the combination of premodern hierarchy and modern equality. Since the fundamental ideals of modern liberalism have been compromised, the only alternative is to conform to a system in which one no longer believes.[13]

My understanding of Neo-Liberal centrism stems from my experience working at universities, which are often shaped by this political ideology. In fact, the contradiction of the contemporary university is that it combines a desire for equality and universal access with an obsession for hierarchy, rankings, and ratings.[14] Driven by the ideology of meritocracy, universities are supposed to promote equal opportunity, but they rely on status, which is revealed by competitive ranking systems, constant grading and evaluation, and professorial ranks.[15] Moreover, this tension between modern equality and premodern hierarchy is often covered by obsessional and narcissistic virtue-signaling where one has to constantly show that one is a good moral person committed to progressive values as one tries to out-compete others for prestige, power, and money.[16] Competitive careerism requires that one learns how to work the system for one's own benefit as one claims that one is performing a public service. This corruption of the public good may be systemic, but it relies on the psychopathology of individuals to sustain it.[17]

In contrast to the defensive centrism described above, a key principle of classic modern liberalism that is often ignored today is that science and democracy are based on critical introspection so that one can become aware of one's own biases.[18] Since the goal is to have an impartial judge of empirical evidence in law and scientific observation, a mode of self-analysis is necessary to achieve neutrality. Just as in psychoanalysis, the neutrality of the analyst allows for the free association of the patient, modern democracy and science begin with the ethical principle of constructed impartiality.[19] Since it is not natural or intuitive to be neutral, this subjective position represents a break with nature and evolution. Freud adds that scientists must also be humble and realize the limits of knowledge as one accepts the necessities of life and the inevitability of conflict.[20] As a moral and ethical principle, the reality principle requires suspending the pursuit of the pleasure principle and the move beyond fantasy and delusion.[21] Unfortunately, these scientific principles are rarely taught as ethical beliefs, and so it is easy to say that science has no morals or meaning. Thus, due in part to the repression of the ethical nature of scientific thinking, people turn to the notion that our society is helplessly corrupt and amoral, and so the only thing one can do is to take advantage of a flawed structure.

For Klein, political as well as social polarization is the main defining aspect of systemic corruption and distortion: "to appeal to a more polarized public, political institutions and political actors behave in more polarized ways. As political institutions and actors become more polarized, they further polarize the public" (xx). In the endless feedback loop of polarization, Klein reveals how the system uses us, and we seek to use the flawed system to our own advantage. Polarization then undermines modern liberal democracy because it eliminates neutrality, universality, and objectivity.[22] Within a structure where everyone is motivated to see things in a binary way, the system becomes more oppositional as people sort themselves into the extreme ends of the political spectrum. Of course, Klein's own discourse caters to this polarization by conforming to the system it critiques and by not offering a true modern liberal alternative.

Klein also takes a very anti-modern, anti-psychoanalytic position by claiming that every political perspective is a form of identity politics (xx). In contrast to this universalizing of identity politics, one of the key moves of psychoanalysis is to suspend identity as a guiding force since the goal of the analysis is to take a neutral perspective on oneself and on others, and this is only possible if one does not base one's views and perceptions on identity and identification.[23] Lacan was fond of showing how the subject of the unconscious has no identity, and what one finds in a dream or verbal slip is a loss of self-control.[24] In terms of modern liberalism, equality and universality require treating everyone the same regardless of their identities and identification, and science is only possible if it is not guided by self-interest or cultural identity.[25]

Polarizing Social Science

The focus on identification and identity in Klein's book is evident in the surveys and social science research he presents. For example, the following reference seeks to detail the level of American political polarization based on specific identity groups: "Democrats and Republicans are now sharply distinguished by a set of basic psychological dispositions related to experiential openness—a general dimension of personality tapping tolerance for threat and uncertainty in one's environment" (43–44). In a rare nod to individual psychology, Klein's source seeks to divide Democrats and Republicans according to their level of openness to new experiences.[26] The first thing I want to point out about this study is that it frames the analysis of political ideologies by the binary opposition between the two main parties, and as we see throughout Klein's book, the binary logic of party affiliation is often conflated with opposed political ideologies and distinct demographic and lifestyle patterns. The overall argument is that just as the two main political parties have becomes more extreme and opposed to each other, so have our belief systems and our life choices. However, a problem with this perspective is that instead of seeing the two parties fighting over five distinct political ideologies (Left, Right, Liberal, Conservative, and Centrist), it tends to reduce ideological differences to a polarized binary, and then it relates this binary to demographic patterns and consumer tendencies.[27] One reason why this reductive analytic lens is possible is that a basic dynamic of American politics is obscured, and this dynamic concerns the way the Republicans have formed a coalition between conservatives and the Right, while Democrats have tried to combine Neo-Liberal centrists and the Left. Each party then caters to more than one ideology, and making matters more complicated is that most Americans usually do not vote, and many declare that they have no party affiliation. It is therefore unclear how one can jump from party voting to lifestyle choices if most people are excluded from the central lens of the party binary.[28] By falling back on party affiliation as the structuring opposition, Klein's analysis and the sources he cites make it virtually impossible not to find high levels of polarization: if you are only giving people two choices, they are going to be seen as having only two perspectives. Therefore, identity politics here is really party affiliation, and this is a very limited way of understanding political ideology.

Another example of this confusion among different analytic lens can be found in the following passage regarding Marc Hetherington and Jonathan Weiler's *Prius or Pickup? How the Answers to Four Simple Questions Explain America's Great Divide*:

> Different studies categorize people in different ways, but the common thread is that openness to experience—and the basic optimism that drives it—is associated with liberalism, while conscientiousness,

> a preference for order and tradition that breeds a skepticism toward disruptive change, connects to conservatism.
>
> (44)

Here the defining opposition is liberal versus conservative, but this distinction leaves out the Left and the Right.[29] It is also unclear if fearfulness and openness align with party affiliation, political ideology, or underlying psychological motivations related to surveys structured to only give participants a binary choice.

It can be quite entertaining to learn that liberals and conservatives like different foods and shop at different stores, but these consumer trends may hide a more complex diversity of political ideologies. As we shall see in Klein's uncritical use of these surveys, there is little consistency in the categories used to frame the research:

> People who score high on openness, for example, tend to like envelope-pushing music and abstract art. People who score high on conscientiousness are more likely to be organized, faithful, and loyal … This is why Whole Foods and Cracker Barrel locations track deep partisan divisions.
>
> (45)

As this passage skips from biology to psychology to consumer choices to political ideology, it provides a totalizing view of a wide range of influences and responses.[30] Even if we are sure that self-identified liberals shop at Whole Foods and are open to trying new things, but conservatives like Cracker Barrel because they believe in traditional values, we have to ask how is liberal and conservative being defined here and how do these two political ideologies relate to the five different ideologies I have articulated? There is also the question of how biology relates to culture and psychology. At times, Klein is jumping from biological determinism to social determinism to psychological determinism, and each approach contradicts the other two. Instead of being presented with a coherent, multi-variable theory, we are shown a combination of distinct perspectives that are then re-packaged as a coherent whole.

Much of the research cited by Klein relies on self-reporting, and here we run into another difference with psychoanalysis. A fundamental principle of psychoanalysis is that people lie to themselves and they lie to others in order to present a positive self-image.[31] Moreover, if people have unconscious motivations, it is unclear how they will be able to access them in simple survey questions, especially questions that have been constructed to give people limited response options.[32] These surveys take on an air of being scientific, but they usually are not validated by the same criteria required by academic research. In fact, currently, many academic studies in the social sciences have failed to be replicated, and this flaw is often due to the way that the researchers let bias define their analysis.[33]

One problem with much of the surveys and research on political preferences stems from the fact that most Americans have no real preference or political involvement (48). Since most Americans do not vote in most elections, and even when they do vote, they often do not have clear policy preferences, our conception of the polarization of politics must be in part due to the fact that some of the people who do vote have strong opinions and strong party preferences, but these people do not make up the majority.[34] The political scientists and people doing political surveys simply exclude the majority of people, and then they focus on the extremes, which creates a strong sense of polarization.

I think that Klein may like presenting this questionable data because it provides a clear and entertaining picture for his audience to consume. However, a side-effect of this discourse is that people begin to see the world in a much more polarized way, and this perspective can lead to more actual polarization. Returning to the psychoanalytic understanding of binary thinking, the unconscious processes of denial, splitting, and projection are driven by a desire to escape tension and complexity, and this escape from anxiety satisfies the goal of the pleasure principle.[35] In the case of centrists, their desire to see themselves as good and knowledgeable makes them seek out sources of information that support their worldview and which draw a clear line between the good us and the evil other. The discourse on polarization, then, feeds this need for splitting between good and evil as it divides the world into extreme opposites.

Like Haidt, Klein's political ideology often combines a use of reason with a rejection of reason. In other words, he makes reasonable claims about the inability of reason to shape our perceptions of the world and ourselves: "What if our loyalties and prejudices are governed by instinct and merely rationalized as calculation?" (50). As a form of liberal irony, one has to rely on the rationality of one's audience in order to convince them that they are not guided by reason.[36] One benefit of making this argument is that if reason cannot control our emotions and instincts, then we are not responsible for what we do and say since these emotions are unconscious biological responses. It is also unclear why Klein would be writing this book if he did not believe that people will accept his reasons as being reasonable and not just some post facto rationalizations. This contradiction points to the idea that ironic centrists have to always come down squarely on two sides of every issue since they want to be free individuals as they conform to social norms. By taking an ironic stance on their own positions, they are able to conform from a position of distance.[37] They therefore cannot be held responsible for what they say or do because they do not directly identify with their own words or actions. As Descartes revealed, when we conform to others, we are able to escape feelings of remorse or anxiety because we are no longer responsible since we are just copying someone else.[38] One reason then why centrists might have a hard time with Leftists is that people on the Left often fully identify with what they are saying and doing.

It should not be surprising that extreme views result in polarized politics, but it is also important to remember that most people do not have extreme political views, and many have no clear view at all.[39] Maybe centrists want to see extreme polarization because they desire to clear a space for the moderate middle, but this center often ends up being defined by an ironic and cynical combination of two opposing perspectives. The middle then does not represent neutrality or universality since the combination of two extreme ideas does not result in the production of an open perspective. On a fundamental basis, modern liberal neutrality is not based on finding a common ground between two extremes: it is about suspending the extremes in an effort to look at facts in an impartial way. Since Klein believes that that system is helplessly corrupt and polarized, there appears to be little chance for real democracy, and yet he does use reason to articulate the failure of reason.

The Rhetoric of the Good Self

This centrist desire to see problems as located in systems and not in our selves is foreground in Klein's discussion of Barak Obama's rhetoric:

> "Even as we speak, there are those who are preparing to divide us," he said, "the spin masters and negative ad peddlers who embrace the politics of anything goes." Notice the rhetorical move Obama makes. We are not divided. We can only be divided. The polarizers are out there. We are their victims, our disagreements their product.
>
> (65)

In saying that we are the victims of polarization, the self remains innocent as the other is seen as being corrupted. This protection of the pure self and the demonization of the evil other plays a key role in contemporary centrist irony. For instance, many centrists love to watch late-night comedy shows that mock politicians and the political system. Humor is used here to create a space where suffering can be turned into pleasure as the comedian escapes criticism by claiming that it is just a joke.[40] In this structure, the self can remain pure as the outside world is critiqued; since the fault is outside, the subject remains a pure and innocent victim. For ironic narcissistic centrists, this protection of the pure self is the essential driving force and pushes them to seek to have their intended virtue recognized by others.[41]

From a psychoanalytic perspective, this post-postmodern type of liberalism relates to the way we demand to have our ideal ego recognized by an ideal Other.[42] Through this obsessional narcissistic transference, the subject wants to be seen as being good by an approving other, and this relation to an imaginary ideal helps to repress feelings of guilt and shame. One reason, then, why some people think that Democrat politicians are fake and manipulative is that their efforts to do good appear to be forced and based on ulterior motives. In fact, Freud went as far as saying that behind every good intention, there is an unconscious evil desire.[43] Lacan added that altruism often comes coupled with a desire to control and debase the other.[44]

It is important to note that I have been forced to use the term "centrist liberal" to indicate that there is a liberal form of Neo-Liberalism, and this type of liberal centrism is very different from classic modern liberalism. While we tend to think of contemporary Neo-Liberalism as only a Right-wing libertarian attack on the welfare states, taxes, postmodern minority-based social movements, and political correctness, there is also a liberal version of this reaction to postmodern identity politics.[45] Instead of simply being insensitive to discrimination and prejudice, post-postmodern centrists usually offer education as the meritocratic solution to social and economic inequality.[46] This investment ignores that our current systems of education often enhance economic inequality and reduce social mobility, but since liberal centrists believe that education can resolve all social problems, they refuse to see how it can make things even worse.[47] Moreover, since centrists are so focused on being seen as doing good by others, they are unable to use science and reality testing to acknowledge the harm done by their own beliefs and policies. These centrist liberals love to say that they are good people and they intend to do good things, but this idealization of the self acts to repress the reality of their underlying aggression and the real effects of their actions.

If we look at how education functions in many countries today, it often works to socialize people to compete for a scarce resource (grades, degrees, ranks) from a position of cynical distance.[48] Since people know that these rewards and ratings are themselves corrupt and corrupting, they compete in a system in which they no longer believe. For example, universities know that college ranking systems are simplistic and misleading, but these same schools spend a great deal of money and time trying to out-compete other schools.[49] Likewise, students may not care about what they are learning, but they still want to get the highest grade. The ultimate goal, thus, of the centrist form of Neo-Liberalism is to train people to be competitive capitalists who do not believe in what they are doing. This system can be seen as beneficial to society because it accomplishes the dual goal of motivating people to work as it renders them disinterested in changing the system. Since these centrist liberals no longer believe in the foundations of modern liberalism, they are able to conform from a position of cynical distance.

We can also understand the centrist tendency to compromise and seek a middle-ground as the effect of the lack of belief in modern liberal democracy and science. This compromising desire is seen in Klein's further analysis of Obama's speech: "There's not a liberal America and a conservative America—there's the United States of America" (65). This desire to see a middle-ground by affirming both extremes and denying the truth of their differences makes Obama appear good and reasonable, but the result of this rhetoric is to simply repress the truth of the situation. In what has been termed "obsessional compliance," liberal narcissists often conform to the demands of others and work as hard as they can to do what the other wants, but this compliance is coupled with a lack of belief.[50] In Obama's efforts to combine premodern religion with modern democracy, he ends up making a superficial call for unity: here polarization is denied as an imaginary unity is proclaimed.

Klein adds that in response to a question about polarization that he asked Obama, the president told him that everyone has a friend or relative from the opposite end of the political spectrum, but we still love them. However, as soon as politics becomes a point of discussion, they exclaim: "I can't believe you think that!" (66). Obama's Neo-Liberal centrist response here is to say that on an everyday level, we can all get along, but it is the political system that makes us feel polarized. However, I have been arguing that political affiliation is driven by ideology, and ideology is itself structured by particular psychopathologies, and so it is hard to separate how people act on a daily basis from their ideologies and ultimately their party affiliations.

The model I am presenting here is centered on the dialectical relation between culture and subjectivity. Just as people with certain personality types are drawn to certain political ideologies and parties, these social organizations and belief systems are themselves structure by particular psychopathological forces. Moreover, in a mutual feedback loop, culture shapes individuals and individuals shape culture, and so we need to think about polarization as both a subjective unconscious process and as a cultural framework. In seeing this dialectic, we can avoid the centrist desire to just wish away polarization or to blame it on others. In fact, another quote from Obama shows that he believes we can move beyond polarization by just choosing a different media strategy: Obama argued that polarized media, gerrymandering, and the flood of political money tended to balkanize us into our political identities.

> "So my advice to a future president," he said, "is increasingly try to bypass the traditional venues that create divisions and try to find new venues within this new media that are quirkier, less predictable."
>
> (68)

While it is very popular now to blame the media for our polarization, it should be clear that our systems of social communication tend to amplify unconscious processes located in all of us. Even if one follows Obama and seeks to find a new media that is less predictable, it is hard to see how this effort will result in a change in the psychopathology of everyday political ideologies. Since these cultural systems take advantage of our own desires, fears, and defense mechanisms, a change in how the media presents political information will not fundamentally alter how we see the world.

Beyond Identity Politics

Klein's response to Obama's strategy returns to the topic of identity politics, which Klein believes is the key to both our subjective and political beliefs and actions:

> he was too optimistic in believing that our nonpolitical identities could become our political identities, that they were somehow a truer reflection of our essential selves, and thus strong enough to overwhelm our partisan divisions. In practice, our political identities are polarizing our other identities, too.
>
> (68)

From Klein's perspective, since political polarization is also polarizing our everyday perceptions of the world and our own selves, then it is impossible to seek out a politics that is not divided by identities. What I think this perspective gets wrong is that it does not allow for the necessary but impossible ideals of modern democracy and science, which are founded on the effort to suspend all personal bias and identity.[51] Since our identities represent conscious and unconscious identifications that have become fixated, the only way to affirm the reality principle is to seek to suspend these fixations through critical introspection. In other words, we do not need more identity politics; rather, we have to find a way outside of this structure. In order to promote universal human rights, we have to suspend the importance of particular identities in favor of universal equality. However, we also should recognize that the only way to make sure that all people will be protected by democratic rights is if we also enable social movements based on particular identities to expand who is covered by universal human rights.[52] There is thus a necessary dialectic between modern democratic equality and postmodern identity politics, yet, problems arise when the postmodern social movements become fixated on their identities and no longer direct their attention towards the goal of equality. Unfortunately, too many centrists do not understand the necessity of this dialectic, and so they simply take for granted the results of social movements without understanding the need for the constant expansion of universal equality.

When we do not see the limitations of identity politics, and we fail to affirm the modern liberal goal of unbiased equal judgment, then we end up like Klein seeing the world as hopelessly polarized and polarizing: "A single vote can now indicate a person's partisan preference as well as his or her religion, race, ethnicity, gender, neighborhood, and favorite grocery store" (68). On the one hand, I think Klein is right to show how our political affiliations can be traced to our identities just as our identities can be related to our political ideologies, but what he does not do is to clearly distinguish the five separate ideologies I have been describing (conservative, liberal, Right, Left, and centrist), and the result is a world shaped purely by a polarization of identity politics.[53] Moreover, by not offering modern liberal democracy as a viable alternative, he becomes trapped in a hall of reflecting mirrors where thoughts about polarization only cause more polarization.

As an example of the limits of identity politics in everyday life, we can look at the educational argument that students should only be taught by people that come from the same demographic group. Many Neo-Liberal universities have adopted this Left-wing perspective by trying to make their faculty more diverse and by trying to make their student body more reflective of local demographics.[54] Although there is nothing inherently wrong in this desire to correct social disparities through social structures, in the case of education, the entire idea of using knowledge and shared methodologies to access the truth of the world and our own selves is undermined by the idea that education is determined by identity and identification. Although it is still important to have identity-based social movements fighting for social justice, when these movements become incorporated into educational and scientific institutions, they can become a distorting force.[55] If we do not want our scientists to be making their discoveries based on their identities or the identities of others, then we should not be basing our educational decisions on demographic factors. Many activists on the Left and centrist moralists will find this argument offensive, but it is vital to understand how modernity developed out of the process of separating the state from the church, the private from the public, the subject from the object, and science from capitalism. These separations are key to the modern liberal social contract, and when we base science and education on identity politics, we lose the fundamental separation between objectivity and subjectivity. Moreover, we need to understand that the core idea behind modern democracy is the ideal of equality, and this ideal has to be determined by an impartial judge.

In their rejection of neutrality, centrists either deny conflict or they see the world in polarized terms. This avoidance of tension is one of the reasons why they generally reject revolution or violent protests: they ultimately do not want to push for radical transformations, and they prefer slow reform over major changes. However, it is vital not to see the center as some rational, non-ideological fact-based discourse. Since the center is a reaction to two ideological extremes, it is shaped by these extremes, and so it remains highly ideological. Although centrists may say they are just promoting common sense, they are ruled by unconscious processes that function to misrepresent the truth. Moreover, since identity plays such a large role in the subjectivity of people who are trying to present and maintain a positive self-image, these identities are easily politicized.[56] In fact, Klein insists that everything can now be seen through the lens of political identities:

> Living in a city, being a liberal, shopping at Trader Joe's, and dabbling in Zen meditation may not have much to do with one another in terms of public policy, but they reinforce a singular identity, and that identity is political, or at least easily politicized.
>
> (69)

Since every identity is subject to politicization, there appears to be no social or subjective space outside of the political.

One result of the apparent politicization of every aspect of human life is that the modern liberal ideal of impartiality is lost. The spread of ideology throughout our culture also means that people do not trust others since everyone is seen as just supporting their own team and rejecting the other side. Centrism does not resolve this problem because it does not clear a space for the non-ideological, which is a necessary but impossible ideal of modern democracy. A paradox, then, of the original model of modern liberalism is that it sought to create a politics beyond political bias or self-interest. Even if this ideal is never fully attained, it still functions to structure many of our social institutions, and when it fails to live up to its own standards, it can always be corrected by being compared to its ideal principles. When we are unable to envision this neutral space, then all we can see is partisan alternatives, and even if it looks like moderate centrists do provide an impartial perspective, we have seen that this is clearly not the case.

As Klein argues, a related issue of our polarized identity-based politics is that people are not voting for particular public policies; instead, they are basing their votes on their identities:

> Interestingly, it turns out that there's only a weak relationship between how much a person identifies as a conservative or liberal and how conservative or liberal their views actually are—to be exact, in both cases it's about a .25 correlation.
>
> (74)

Although Klein does not clearly define what he means by identity, it appears to be centered on the way people see themselves through a limited set of cultural signifiers. This conception of identity is itself highly narcissistic since it is centered on the identification with preferred social values in a structure where the outside world acts as a mirror containing ideal representations of the self and the other.[57] Unfortunately, Klein's analysis tends to avoid any explanation of subjectivity and completely avoids some of the key principles of psychoanalysis, which are that we often are not aware of our own intentions or investments, and even our identities can be unconscious or self-deceiving. Moreover, since our ego is formed out of internalized identifications with traits we see in others, we are often unaware of our own beliefs or desires.[58] A problem then with his focus on identity politics is that identity is understood as a simple form of conscious self-awareness.

In a revealing moment, Klein confesses that his research on polarization and identity-based politics has forced him to give up his previous belief in the role of reason in politics:

> My whole career—and much of politics more generally—is based on the idea that gathering good information helps us understand hard policy issues and that putting the two together can change minds and lead to a better world. But once our political identities and interests push themselves in front of our cognition, that model of reasoning falls to pieces.
>
> (102)

According to this perspective, the fact that we are guided by our identities and not by factual information means that there is little reason to try to be scientific or rational when discussing or analyzing politics. As I have been arguing, this replacement of reason with bias is exactly what undermines our ability to pursue modern science and democracy.

What clearly differentiates modern liberalism from current centrism is that contemporary centrists no longer believe in the value of trying to promote the principles of impartiality, universality, objectivity, and reason. However, while at times, Klein does dismiss the role of reason in politics and political identities, at other times, he appears to defend its importance: "the fact that our capacities for rationality seem to have evolved as a by-product of other capabilities, like language—underscores how precious the ability to reason is and how attentive we must be to its development" (102). Here, reason is valorized as Klein insists that we must understand its limits, but we should also see it as a precious gift. It is thus strange that for most of his work on polarization and identity, reason is dismissed since it cannot compete with our intuitive identification and motivated cognition.

By focusing on politicized identities, Klein falls into the trap of suspending reason by focusing on superficial demographic identity markers: "A useful rule of thumb is that political power runs a decade behind demographics, with older, whiter, more Christian voters turning out at higher rates" (111). Just as Left-wing social movements can become fixated on their own identity and not the goal of universality and equal justice, the obsession with demographic traits undermines the desire for universal human rights. In a polarizing discourse about polarization, politicized identities prevent us from pursuing impersonal universal law. Since we want everyone to be equal in front of the law, then we have to suspend our demographic identities to achieve this universality. In fact, in later chapters, I will stress how we can think of globalization itself as the politics of the universal, and this politics requires transcending polarizing identity politics.

Notes

1 Kramer, Ueli, et al. "Beyond splitting: Observer-rated defense mechanisms in borderline personality disorder." *Psychoanalytic Psychology* 30.1 (2013): 3.
2 Samuels, Robert. "Auto-modernity after postmodernism: Autonomy and automation in culture, technology, and education." *Digital youth, innovation, and the unexpected.* Ed. Tara McPherson. MIT Press (2008).
3 Samuels, Robert. "Catharsis: The politics of enjoyment." *Zizek and the Rhetorical Unconscious.* Palgrave Macmillan, 2020, 7–31.
4 Roy-Chowdhury, Sim. "Is there a place for individual subjectivity within a social constructionist epistemology?" *Journal of Family Therapy* 32.4 (2010): 342–357.
5 Žižek, Slavoj. *The sublime object of ideology.* Verso, 1989.
6 Hennig-Thurau, Thorsten, and Mark B. Houston. *Entertainment science.* Springer Books, 2019.
7 Doherty, Brian. *Radicals for capitalism: A freewheeling history of the modern American libertarian movement.* PublicAffairs, 2009.
8 Tennen, Howard, and Glenn Affleck. "Blaming others for threatening events." *Psychological Bulletin* 108.2 (1990): 209.
9 Cole, Alyson Manda. *The cult of true victimhood: From the war on welfare to the war on terror.* Stanford University Press, 2007.
10 Freud, Sigmund. "The aetiology of hysteria." *April* 21 (1896): 251–282.
11 Marcks, Holger, and Janina Pawelz. "From myths of victimhood to fantasies of violence: How far-right narratives of imperilment work." *Terrorism and Political Violence* (2020): 1–18.
12 Magill, R. Jay. *Chic ironic bitterness.* University of Michigan Press, 2009.
13 Sloterdijk, Peter. *Critique of cynical reason.* Trans. Michael Eldred. Minneapolis: University of Minnesota Press, 1988).
14 Samuels, Robert. *Educating inequality: Beyond the political myths of higher education and the job market.* Taylor & Francis, 2017.
15 Sandel, Michael J. *The tyranny of merit: What's become of the common good?* Allen Lane, 2020.
16 Samuels, Robert. "(Liberal) Narcissism." *Routledge handbook of psychoanalytic political theory.* Routledge, 2019, 151–161.
17 Hedges, Chris. *Death of the liberal class.* Vintage Books Canada, 2011.
18 Pagden, Anthony. *The enlightenment: And why it still matters.* Oxford University Press, 2013.
19 Samuels, Robert. "Logos, global justice, and the reality principle." *Zizek and the rhetorical unconscious.* Palgrave Macmillan, 2020, 65–86.
20 Freud, Sigmund. *Totem and taboo: Resemblances between the psychic lives of savages and neurotics.* Good Press, 2019.

21 Rieff, Philip. *Freud: The mind of the moralist*. University of Chicago Press, 1979.

22 Talisse, Robert B. *Overdoing democracy: Why we must put politics in its place*. Oxford University Press, 2019.

23 Samuels, Robert. *Zizek and the rhetorical unconscious: Global politics, philosophy, and subjectivity*. Springer Nature, 2020.

24 Miller, Jacques-Alain, ed. *The seminar of Jacques Lacan: Book 1: Freud's papers on technique 1953–1954*. CUP Archive, 1988.

25 Rozin, Paul. "The weirdest people in the world are a harbinger of the future of the world." *Behavioral and Brain Sciences* 33.2–3 (2010): 108.

26 Johnston, Christopher D., Howard G. Lavine, and Christopher M. Federico. *Open versus closed: Personality, identity, and the politics of redistribution*. Cambridge University Press, 2017.

27 Wetherell, Margaret. "Beyond binaries." *Theory & Psychology* 9.3 (1999): 399–406.

28 Powell Jr, G. Bingham. "American voter turnout in comparative perspective." *The American Political Science Review* (1986): 17–43.

29 Hetherington, Marc, and Jonathan Weiler. *Prius or pickup?: How the answers to four simple questions explain America's great divide*. Houghton Mifflin, 2018.

30 Hibbing, John R., Kevin B. Smith, and John R. Alford. *Predisposed: Liberals, conservatives, and the biology of political differences*. Routledge, 2013.

31 Freud, Sigmund. "Repression." *The standard edition of the complete psychological works of Sigmund Freud, volume XIV (1914–1916): On the history of the psycho-analytic movement, papers on metapsychology and other works*. Eds. James Strachey and Anna Freud. London: Hogarth Press, 1957: 141–158.

32 Fryer, Luke K., and Kaori Nakao. "The future of survey self-report: An experiment contrasting Likert, VAS, slide, and swipe touch interfaces." *Frontline Learning Research* 8.3 (2020): 10–25.

33 Shrout, Patrick E., and Joseph L. Rodgers. "Psychology, science, and knowledge construction: Broadening perspectives from the replication crisis." *Annual Review of Psychology* 69 (2018): 487–510.

34 Callander, Steven, and Catherine H. Wilson. "Turnout, polarization, and Duverger's law." *The Journal of Politics* 69.4 (2007): 1047–1056.

35 Freud, Sigmund. "Formulations on the two principles of mental functioning." *The standard edition of the complete psychological works of Sigmund Freud, volume XII (1911–1913): The case of Schreber, papers on technique and other works*. 1958, 213–226.

36 Renegar, Valerie R., and Stacey K. Sowards. "Liberal irony, rhetoric, and feminist thought: A unifying third wave feminist theory." *Philosophy & Rhetoric* 36.4 (2003): 330–352.

37 Samuels, Robert. "Beyond Hillary Clinton: Obsessional Narcissism and the failure of the liberal class." *Psychoanalyzing the left and right after Donald Trump*. Palgrave Macmillan, 2016, 31–59.

38 Descartes, René, and Donald A. Cress. *Discourse on method*. Hackett Publishing, 1998.

39 Strandberg, Thomas, et al. "Depolarizing American voters: Democrats and republicans are equally susceptible to false attitude feedback." *Plos one* 15.2 (2020): e0226799.
40 Contu, Alessia. "Decaf resistance: On misbehavior, cynicism, and desire in liberal workplaces." *Management Communication Quarterly* 21.3 (2008): 364–379.
41 Samuels, Robert. "Transference and Narcissism." *Freud for the twenty-first century*. Palgrave Pivot, 2019, 43–51.
42 Lacan, Jacques. *The ego in Freud's theory and in the technique of psychoanalysis, 1954–1955*. Vol. 2. WW Norton & Company, 1991.
43 Freud, Sigmund. "Notes upon a case of obsessional neurosis." *The standard edition of the complete psychological works of Sigmund Freud, volume X (1909): Two case histories ('Little Hans' and the 'Rat Man')*. Eds. James Strachey and Anna Freud. London: Hogarth Press, 1955, 151–318.
44 Lacan, Jacques, Alan Sheridan, and Malcolm Bowie. "Aggressivity in psychoanalysis." *Écrits: A selection*. Routledge, 2020, 9–32.
45 Aalbers, Manuel B. "Debate on Neoliberalism in and after the neoliberal crisis." *International Journal of Urban and Regional Research* 37.3 (2013): 1053–1057.
46 Marsh, John. *Class dismissed: Why we cannot teach or learn our way out of inequality*. NYU Press, 2011.
47 Samuels, Robert. *Educating inequality: Beyond the political myths of higher education and the job market*. Taylor & Francis, 2017.
48 Samuels, Robert. "Ethos, transference, and liberal cynicism." *Zizek and the Rhetorical Unconscious*. Palgrave Macmillan, 2020, 49–63.
49 Michael, Steve O. "The cost of excellence: The financial implications of institutional rankings." *The International Journal of Educational Management* 19.5 (2005): 365–382.
50 Salkovskis, Paul M. "Obsessional-compulsive problems: A cognitive-behavioural analysis." *Behaviour Research and Therapy* 23.5 (1985): 571–583.
51 Laclau, Ernesto, and Chantal Mouffe. *Hegemony and socialist strategy: Towards a radical democratic politics*. Verso Trade, 2014.
52 Samuels, Robert. "Logos, global justice, and the reality principle." *Zizek and the rhetorical unconscious*. Palgrave Macmillan, 2020, 65–86.
53 Mason, Lilliana. *Uncivil agreement: How politics became our identity*. University of Chicago Press, 2018.
54 Michaels, Walter Benn. *The trouble with diversity: How we learned to love identity and ignore inequality*. Macmillan, 2016.
55 Samuels, Robert. *Teaching writing, rhetoric, and reason at the Globalizing University*. Routledge, 2020.
56 Stout, Christopher T. *The case for identity politics: Polarization, demographic change, and racial appeals*. University of Virginia Press, 2020.
57 Lacan, Jacques. "The mirror stage as formative of the function of the I as revealed in psychoanalytic experience." *Cultural Theory and Popular Culture. A Reader*. London: Routledge, 2014, 287–292.
58 Freud, Sigmund. *Mass psychology*. Penguin UK, 2004.

4 Understanding the Psychopathology of the Right

Corey Robin's *The Reactionary Mind: Conservatism from Edmund Burke to Donald Trump* endeavors to trace the intellectual history of Right-wing political ideology from the early modern period to the current age. However, in his effort to provide a connection between conservative thought and Donald Trump, he ends up mystifying both conservativism and the libertarian Right. We shall see that due to his lack of understanding of the psychopathology of these discrete political movements, he is unable to explain how someone like Trump became president.[1] Interestingly, by focusing on the history of ideas, he is blind to the role played by unconscious forces shaping both subjectivity and cultural formations.

The Difference between Conservatives and the Right

Due to Robin's desire to connect current Right-wing politics to conservative ideology, he has to separate conservativism from its roots in premodern religion. For instance, in the following passage, we see how he confuses conservativism and the Right-wing backlash against progressive social movements:

> many of the characteristics we have come to associate with contemporary conservatism—racism, populism, violence, and a pervasive contempt for custom, convention, law, institutions, and established elites—are not recent or eccentric developments of the American right. They are instead constitutive elements of conservatism, dating back to its origins in the European reaction against the French Revolution. From its inception, conservatism has relied upon some mix of these elements to build a broad-based movement of elites and masses against the emancipation of the lower orders.
>
> (xi)

DOI: 10.4324/9781003199649-4

What is so misleading in this summary of his own work is that he does not distinguish between, on the one hand, the premodern belief in a rigid social hierarchy based primarily on religion, and on the other hand, the post-postmodern backlash against revolutions, minority-based social movements, and the creation of the welfare state.[2] On a fundamental basis, conservatives seek to conserve an already existing social hierarchy, while Right-wing reactionaries reject the results of progressive social revolutions. Moreover, a key aspect of the French Revolution is the promotion of the modern break from premodernity, and this break is centered on the democratic and secular ideals of universal justice.[3] It is vital to make these historical distinctions because there is a tendency to confuse different political ideologies. Although premodern conservatives did use a form of racism and social prejudice to justify the exploitation of the lower classes, it would be wrong to see this ideology as being anti-elite or anti-institution.

One reason why I think it is so essential to clearly differentiate between conservative and Right-wing ideology is that we have to understand that the current Republican coalition is based on a contradictory combination of opposing forces. For instance, not only is Trump clearly not a religious conservative, but his lack of respect for the law and other social institutions places him at odds with the foundations of conservative ideology.[4] The question, then, becomes how is he able to receive the support of conservatives when he so clearly does not represent their values? The short answer to this question is that American conservatives have simply taken the pragmatic choice of using Trump to achieve their agenda, and as many conservatives have said, sometimes the messenger conflicts with the true message.[5] While Robin does not spend much time on the religious foundation of most conservative ideologies, it should be clear that religious fundamentalism around the world and throughout history is often centered on conserving a social hierarchy that privileges men over women and the powerful over the disempowered.[6] From this perspective, conservativism has always been about social power, and so it should not be surprising if conservative ideologues would use someone like Trump to realize their agenda. Not only is Trump an amoral opportunist who can be motivated to endorse any ideological position if it helps him to gain and maintain power, but conservative Christians themselves often use religious beliefs to hide their true motivations, which is to impose their will on others.[7] From this perspective, conservative ideas are just a post facto rationalization of power dynamics.

While in the previous chapter, I focused on the problems that ensue when centrists debase the role of reason in politics in order to focus on identity and polarization, in this chapter, I want to examine how the focus on ideas and philosophy can blind us from understanding how power functions to determine the psychopathology of conservative and libertarian politics. Furthermore, the conservative quest to maintain inherited social hierarchies is very different from the libertarian desire to be free from all social constraints, and yet the two ideologies are able to work together because they are both centered on issues concerning social power.[8] From a psychoanalytic perspective, a key aspect of conservative ideology is the paradoxical combination of authority and submission. On one level, it should be clear that premodern societies are determined by social hierarchies functioning to give certain groups of people power over others, and yet on another level, even the people with power see their social position as determined by faith, fate, and belief.[9] Since the social hierarchy is inherited and predetermined, everyone must submit to a cultural hierarchy that is already there. This submission can be seen in terms of masochism since people have to identify with a structure that is outside of their control as they turn their suffering into pleasure and their amorality into a moral rationalization.[10]

Conservative Moral Masochism

To understand the masochistic psychopathology of conservative ideology, we can look at Lacan's theory of the discourse of the master, which posits that even the master is subjected to a pre-existing social order, which is itself structured by a set of symbolic social oppositions.[11] A clear example of this discourse can be found in Aristotle's *Politics*, where he seeks to justify the master's rule of the slave:

> For the soul rules the body with a despotical rule, whereas the intellect rules the appetites with a constitutional and royal rule. And it is clear that the rule of the soul over the body, and of the mind and the rational element over the passionate, is natural and expedient; whereas the equality of the two or the rule of the inferior is always hurtful. The same holds good of animals in relation to men; for tame animals have a better nature than wild, and all tame animals are better off when they are ruled by man; for then they are preserved. Again, the male is by nature superior, and the female inferior; and the one rules, and the other is ruled; this principle, of necessity, extends to all mankind.
>
> (19)[12]

Aristotle, here, lists a set of oppositions and hierarchies that still function to structure conservative ideologies today: men over women, the mind over the body, reason over emotions, humans over animals, and the tame over the untamed. This series of symbolic binary oppositions sets up a system of structured hierarchies that reinforce each other, and as Lacan argues, we see here how the discourse of the master is constituted through the use of symbolic differences and analogies that are then taken to be natural and therefore inevitable.[13]

Although we may believe that we have moved past this premodern structure, it should be clear that many of these oppositions still shape our world today, and what in part makes people conservative is that they are dedicated to conserving predefined social hierarchies.[14] Ultimately, the driving force behind this ideology is the desire of men to control other people by getting them to submit to a structure that oppresses them. While Aristotle stresses the way this system is sustained because it is natural and therefore inevitable, it should be clear that this philosopher's rationalization of oppression hides the role played by the threat of symbolic violence in motivating people to accept the social hierarchy.[15] For psychoanalysis, this threat is called castration, and it is important to view it as an imagined bodily dismembering, even though actual violence often plays a role in sustaining the system.[16] As a fundamental form of patriarchy, this privileging of men over women is generated in part by the threat of violence that forces all subjects to submit to the structure.[17] Moreover, since this threat has to be internalized on a subjective level, it must be symbolic even if it is the result of a real event.[18]

In utilizing this psychoanalytic theory of the conservative discourse of the master, we will see that Robin also ends up idealizing and distorting this ideology. Not only does he confuse conservativism with libertarianism, but he misses the role played by internalized violence in the maintenance of conservative ideology. An example of this confusion can be found in the following passage:

> Rooted in its opposition to the Soviet Union, the labor movement, the welfare state, feminism, and civil rights, conservatism had achieved most of its basic goals as set by the benchmarks of the New Deal, the 1960s, and the Cold War.
>
> (xii)

What Robin is describing here is clearly the backlash against the postmodern welfare state and Left-wing social movements, but these reactionary movements should not be considered to be conservative.[19] Although some on the Right may say that they are seeking to return to a conservative order where everyone knows their place, for the most part, reactionaries are defined by what they are against, while conservatives focus on preserving a social order that is structured by a set of internal oppositions. Moreover, the Right's ideology is focused on individual freedom, while conservatives stress the need for everyone to submit to a predetermined social hierarchy.[20] Furthermore, for this social hierarchy to be conserved, it has to be structured by clear symbolic oppositions enforced through the traumatic threat of bodily harm.[21]

According to Freud's theory of the castration complex, the male child responds to a parental threat by identifying with the source of the threat.[22] Moreover, the super-ego is thus formed through the internalization of authority with an identification with the aggressor.[23] This model of moral masochism means that one submits to the social hierarchy by turning violence into obedience.[24] Likewise, within the structure of a gendered hierarchy, women become the object of social exchange, which further organizes the social order, and their submission is also fortified through real and symbolic violence.[25] One reason then why most religions are also highly patriarchic is that gender oppositions are a clear way of structuring and policing seemingly natural differences.[26] Just like men, women have to submit to their subordination, but women are doubly submitted since they not only have to accept the pre-existing social hierarchy, but this hierarchy places them in a position of inferiority.

True conservative ideology, therefore, has to be seen as a form of patriarchy and gender discrimination.[27] Moreover, this naturalization of the gender hierarchy is coupled with the internalization of a set of racial, class, and ethnic prejudices reinforcing the conservation of the discourse of the master. It is thus very telling that Aristotle seeks to justify slavery by looking at gender, which is itself related to the privileging of humans over animals and the mind over the body. Since Aristotle is a free wealthy white male, he believes that his attributes are superior, while the opposite attributes are inferior.[28] Furthermore, due to the fact that we structure our social systems through the process of splitting and denial, the polarized division between the superior master and the inferior slave points to the way that the people in power project their own debased traits onto others, and then they attack these others for being inferior.[29] It is vital to stress that this theory of the premodern discourse of the master predates modern capitalism, and so it is misleading to tie the origins of racism and sexism to capitalism. In fact, Marx insisted that what in part defines modern capitalism is the melting away of premodern traditions and patriarchy.[30] From this perspective, once exchange value replaces moral values, conservative ideologies are also undermined. In fact, we shall see that one of the things that differentiate conservativism from free-market libertarianism is that the latter ideology is determined by amoral opportunism and not a moral hierarchy.[31]

The Right Trump Card

Robin's failure to clearly comprehend the psychopathology of conservative and Right-wing ideologies blocks him from understanding how someone like Trump could have become president. However, at times, he does see that Trump is in actuality a clear product of the libertarian Right:

> Trump ran on a similar set of anti-establishment themes—he was not tied to the old regime; he had the populist touch; he would thumb his nose at the Republican pooh-bahs and liberal elites; he would vanquish the demons of political correctness; he would bust up the constraining norms of feminism and anti-racism.
>
> (xiii)

As a backlash against Left-wing ideology, Trump appealed to the counterrevolutionary desire to reject postmodern, minority-based social movements, and while his reactionary rhetoric could be seen as a return to conservative ideology, it should be clear that his discourse is defined purely in opposition to the Left.[32] In other words, to understand Trump's ideology, you have to understand the Left's ideology, which itself is centered on trying to reverse premodern conservative hierarchies and prejudices.[33] For example, Trump's sexism is not based on his commitment to religious patriarchy; instead, he seeks to counter the women's movement for equal rights by showing that he will not conform to their progressive ideals.[34] By focusing on political correctness, Trump feeds the libertarian desire for freedom from social constraint and censorship, but this liberation is a liberation from the Left and not a submission to the conservative discourse of the master.[35]

Since Robin does not have a psychoanalytic and historical model of political ideology, he does not see how Trump embodies the libertarian Right (xiii). While Robin thinks Trump has been unable to accomplish the political goals of the Republican party, the opposite is actually the case: no contemporary Republican president has been better at realizing the goals of both conservatives and libertarians. Not only has he supplied conservatives with two conservative Supreme Court justices and hundreds of other federal judges, but he has also provided huge tax cuts for the libertarians as he has also fed premodern prejudices through his racist and anti-immigrant rhetoric.[36] Moreover, he unintentionally displayed that what the conservative religious movement is really about is power. By having a devout Christian as his vice president, he was able to show on a daily basis that in their effort to impose their will on others, these conservatives will tolerate an amoral capitalist as their leader.[37] Mike Pence is then a walking symbol of Christian humiliation and submission, and his born-again narrative shows that in the process of submitting his will to the lord, he has chosen submission over his own reality testing and subjectivity.[38]

What is so scary about Pence for many people is that he appears to really believe in his beliefs, and this level of fundamentalism has the perverse effect of freeing him from any real morality or rationality.[39] Thus, even though he has submitted to Christian moral ideology, this morality allows him a level of predetermined self-righteous certainty placing him in a superior position to all others.[40] As Zizek has argued, one reason why we have so many Catholic priests who are pedophiles is that the belief in the moral value of one's mission frees oneself to do as one pleases.[41] The reason why many conservative politicians, therefore, end up being guilty of the very things they rail against is not only that their politics is a reaction to their own guilt and shame, but they feel that their moral superiority gives them the right to abuse people who are seen as being inferior. We see this same dynamic when Islamic fighters rape women or burn down their places of worship: the people who submit to a higher power tend to believe that they do not have to conform to conventional morality.[42] Pence and other Evangelical Christians can support someone like Trump because their focus is on imposing their morality on others as they unconsciously identify with amoral opportunism.

This focus on power in conservative ideology is highlighted by Robin when he traces the movement of this political belief system:

> Conservatism is the theoretical voice of this animus against the agency of the subordinate classes. It provides the most consistent and profound argument as to why the lower orders should not be allowed to exercise their independent will, why they should not be allowed to govern themselves or the polity. Submission is their first duty, and agency the prerogative of the elite.
>
> (7)

From Robin's perspective, conservative ideology is focused on getting the subordinate classes to submit to the elite by convincing them to give up their independent will. What this interpretation misses is that elites themselves have to submit to a higher order, and this submission is generated out of a threat of violence and the pleasure of conformity. Thus, even if the conservative elites reap the benefits of their position in the social hierarchy, they are socialized to see the world in terms of faith, fate, and belief, which means that they are not using reason or testing reality; instead, through the adherence to a predetermined social order, these conservatives are freed from any real sense of responsibility since everything has already been decided by a higher power and a natural order.[43]

Freud attempted to explain this conservative dynamic by comparing hypnosis to passionate love and the formation of religious and military groups.[44] What he found in all of these diverse relationships is that one submits to the will of other by suspending one's own ability to test reality. By handing over all responsibility to the other, one is free to engage in criminal acts. From this perspective, love is not only deaf and blind, but it also can lead to social transgressions since the lover will do whatever the beloved wants.[45] It is therefore not by accident that there have been so many religious wars and violent acts committed by religious people; just as members of a cult or gang will commit crimes if they are told to do so, when people are put in a social relationship of submission, they are able to deny their own freedom and responsibility, and this liberates them from underlying feelings of guilt and shame.[46] Although we are used to seeing religion as inducing high levels of guilt, these authoritarian structures also allow people to displace guilt and sin onto others. After all, Christians believe that Jesus was sacrificed so that he could pay for the sins of others. As a fundamental mode of transference, religion can give people the ability to transfer their own responsibility and sinful feelings onto an idealized Other.[47]

Revisiting the Five Ideologies

Robin not only often fails to distinguish religious conservatism from Right-wing libertarianism, but he also tends to confuse the Left with liberalism:

> Though it is often claimed that the left stands for equality while the right stands for freedom, this notion misstates the actual disagreement between right and left. Historically, the conservative has favored liberty for the higher orders and constraint for the lower orders.
>
> (8)

It should be first pointed out that modern liberalism is focused on equality, while the Left is often centered on building solidarity around a minority group that has been oppressed by conservative hierarchies.[48] Likewise, the Right does focus on the freedom and liberty of the individual in response to the demands of the Left, but it would be incorrect to equate this desire for freedom to the conservative rejection of equality. For true conservatives, equality is not even in the picture since their worldview is structured by a set of inter-linking social hierarchies.[49] Furthermore, the libertarian Right often sees freedom as a constant-sum game where one's group increased liberty means a decrease in someone else's; in contrast, conservatives are more concerned about submission than freedom.

One reason why I am focusing on how Robin misrepresents these ideologies is that his misconceptions reflect the way many other people fail to understand the underlying structures of political ideologies. By trying to see these belief systems as both subjective and social psychopathologies, I seek to clarify how they work and how they come into being because if we do not understand their structures, we will continue to misunderstand how political ideologies function in the world today. Since political ideologies have a subjective aspect, our comprehension of these shared belief systems can also help us to better see our own internal unconscious processes. Ultimately, the hope is that by making unconscious processes conscious, we can make our relation to ourselves and our world more rational.

By not delving into the underlying psychological processes supporting people's commitments to particular ideologies, Robin is able to view the movement from conservatism to Right-wing libertarianism as an intellectual continuum based on the ideas of early modern thinkers, like Edmund Burke: "'The levellers,' he claimed, 'only change and pervert the natural order of things'" (8). What should be clear from this interpretation of Burke is that this early modern philosopher was reacting to the modern liberal goal of equality. Since he wanted to protect the natural order of things by insisting that people respect authority and the commands of the higher ups, his discourse points to the conservative desire to maintain the premodern social hierarchy, and yet he also focused on reversing the revolutionary demands of the working class.

For Robin, an underlying aspect of conservative ideology is the desire to control private relationships: "Behind the riot in the street or debate in Parliament is the maid talking back to her mistress, the worker disobeying her boss" (10). Robin reveals here the close relationship between patriarchy and conservative ideology; according to this view, what really drives the desire for social order is the desire of men to control the women in their homes and the workers in their workplaces.[50] The discourse of the master is then really a discourse of private power, which relies on the pre-established social hierarchy to rationalize the exploitation of others, but as I discussed above, even the master is subordinate to the system.

Robin adds that the master was so identified with his social position of being a master that any resistance by slaves and subordinates was seen as a threat to the master's identity: "Living every day with his mastery, he became entirely identified with it. So complete was this identification that any sign of the slave's disobedience—much less her emancipation—was seen as an intolerable assault upon his person" (12). Here we see how subjectivity and social structure meet through the construction and maintenance of identity. Since the master's identity is in part defined in opposition to the slave's subordination, the master is reliant on the slave not demonstrating any individual freedom, but this does not mean that the master's identity is defined by the slave's recognition of the master's identity since the master sees the slave as lacking reason and freedom.[51] After all, how can someone without the freedom to judge and think affirm the identity of anyone?[52] The conservative discourse is thus not based on reciprocity, reason, or freedom; rather, this discourse of power and submission circumvents rationality and reality testing, and so when we seek to see conservativism as a part of progressive intellectual history, we are often further obfuscating its true foundation. Since conservative ideas are only after-the-fact rationalization of exploitation, submission, power, and violence, it becomes difficult to discuss the discourse of master using the tools of modern reason.[53]

Even though Robin lacks a psychoanalytic understanding of the structures supporting conservative ideology, he is able to locate the role of private power in this discourse:

> Conservatism, then, is not a commitment to limited government and liberty—or a wariness of change, a belief in evolutionary reform, or a politics of virtue … When the libertarian looks out upon society, he does not see isolated individuals; he sees private, often hierarchical, groups, where a father governs his family and an owner his employees. (16)

This effort to equate conservative and libertarian ideology ends up misrepresenting both. While conservatives do believe that power structures have to be maintained to keep private and social order, libertarians seek to be free from these constraints, and so they are fundamentally opposed to conservatives, and yet the Republicans have found a way to united both groups.[54]

One of the ways that conservatives and libertarians have both been able to support someone like Trump is that both groups are motivated out of their hatred for liberals and the Left. In fact, Republicans want to collapse the difference between liberalism and Left-wing politics so they can unify their coalition around the shared rejection of the opposition.[55] On one level, this structure makes sense because modern liberalism was generated out of a rejection of premodern conservative ideology, while the postmodern Left has sought to reverse the hierarchies structuring premodern conservative ideology. However, as we have seen, the conservative–libertarian coalition is not only defined by its opposition to the Left-liberal coalition but also unified by its focus on a pragmatic consideration of power. Conservatives and Right-wing ideologies realize that they need each other to gain power, and so even if their fundamental beliefs are in conflict with each other, they can accomplish both of their goals by uniting.[56] In contrast, the Left-liberal coalition should have a much harder time because they often value morality over pragmatic power considerations.[57] Many times, it appears that centrist liberals and people on the Left would rather be seen as being morally pure than imposing their will. The paradox here is that the hyper-moralistic conservatives are willing to sacrifice their morals to gain power, while the Left often refuses to give up its sense of being morally superior.[58] Likewise, centrist liberals want to avoid conflict and desire to be seen as having good intentions, and so they are also resistant to seek power for power's sake.

Rewriting History

Since Robin desires to connect early modern conservative ideology to current libertarian politics, he has to rewrite history and locate the birth of conservatism in the modern period: "From the moment conservatism came onto the scene, it has had to contend with the decline of ancient and medieval ideas of an orderly universe, in which permanent hierarchies of power reflected the eternal structure of the cosmos" (18). One of the problems with this version of history is that it separates conservative ideology from premodern religion, feudalism, and monarchy, which in turn obscures the foundations of modern liberalism.[59] I believe it would be more correct to say that contemporary conservatives are derived from the premodern belief in the divine and natural order, while libertarians have little need for a higher power since they are focused on freedom and liberation from authority. Moreover, the liberal response to the premodern is to replace religion with science, monarchy with democracy, and feudalism with capitalism, and so it makes no sense to see conservatism as located in the downfall of the Ancient or Medieval worldviews.[60] In fact, I have used Aristotle's Ancient Greek discourse of the master to show the origins of conservative ideology, which is the dominant belief system from Ancient to Medieval times. When we get this history wrong, we are unable to see the importance and power of modern liberalism as we obscure the difference between conservative and libertarian ideologies.

Once again, I want to stress that this history is not a purely academic debate since it helps us to understand our own politics and identities. However, this effort at understanding is blocked when people like Robin misrepresent the foundations of distinct ideologies. For example, in the following passage he seeks to convince his audience that conservatism is not founded on traditionalism: "Conservatism 'becomes conscious and reflective when other ways of life and thought appear on the scene, against which it is compelled to take up arms in the ideological struggle'" (23). The argument here is that conservatism is always a backlash movement, but this logic equates conservative ideologies with libertarian ones, which is exactly what the Republican party is trying to accomplish through a combination of opposites. In other words, Robin's critique of the Right actually rationalizes the Republican coalition by replacing power relations with post facto moral reasoning. Just as centrists and Leftists want to see the world in terms of the conflict between the good us and the evil other, Robin translates the pragmatic opportunism of the Republican party into a consideration of the intellectual foundation of the movement. Since he does not take into account the irrational and unconscious factors shaping the Right, he ends up seeing this movement as guided by rational and conscious intentions.

One possible reason for this repression of the psychopathology of political ideology is that academic thinkers like to pretend that there must be a moral order to the universe where justice ultimately will prevail. Instead of seeing justice as the product of necessary but impossible ideals housed in social institutions, the academic mind wants to believe that there is a natural moral order. As a form of magical thinking and obsessional superstition, the desire to escape from contingency and unknowability pushes thinkers to imagine that there is a secret order to things.[61] Thus, correlations must have causation, and justice must prevail through some hidden force. Rather than affirming the modern realization that we must make justice happen through the social construction of democratic institutions, a type of moral karma underlies the centrist ideology. Similar to the belief in meritocracy, there is a desire to imagine a just system that rewards people for their knowledge and hard work, and in this way, the role of luck, power, and privilege are repressed.[62]

One place where Robin uses psychology to distinguish political ideologies is in his discussion of what separates conservatives from traditionalists:

> Where the traditionalist can take the objects of desire for granted—he can enjoy them as if they are at hand because they are at hand—the conservative cannot. He seeks to enjoy them precisely as they are being—or have been—taken away.
>
> (23)

The first problem with this analysis is that it claims that there is an opposition between conservativivism and tradition, while it should be clear that a defining aspect of conservative ideology is the effort to conserve traditional values and social hierarchies.[63] The second problem is that his argument is centered on the notion that traditionalists can directly access their objects of desire, but conservatives only desire objects that are taken away. From a psychoanalytic perspective, desire is always based on the loss of objects since one only desires what one does not have.[64] Furthermore, for humans, there is no direct access to reality since everything is mediated by language and consciousness. Unlike other animals, we are only partially shaped by inherited programs directed towards specific objects, and so our desires and drives are always open and mediated. As Lacan insists, pure innocent bliss is impossible for the speaking being because language and society are based in part on the separation from nature and reality.[65] Robin's insistence that traditionalists have some direct access to the objects of their desire must be seen as an idealized fantasy of some original state of human unity with the world.

In contrast to this mystification of traditional desire, Robin does relate conservative desire to the conflict between language and the real: "But as soon as those objects enter the medium of political speech, they cease to be items of lived experience and become incidents of an ideology" (23). Although Robin wants to argue that traditionalists can somehow directly access the objects of their desire but conservatives cannot, it should be clear that all social beings have to mediate their desires through cultural ideologies. In fact, a defining aspect of ideology is that it not only tells us what objects we should not pursue, but also informs us about what objects we should desire.[66] Since, as Freud insists, societies are founded on the need to regulate sexuality and violence, they are centered on the mediation of our natural impulses.[67]

One reason why Robin may fantasize that traditionalists have direct access to the objects they desire is that contemporary centrist liberals love to imagine that their cultural others have the privilege of unmediated sexuality and violence.[68] Thus, the centrist form of racism often involves idealizing the other as one who has escaped from the necessary sacrifices caused by being civilized. We see this type of racism when moderate liberals idealize black men as being great at sports and sex.[69] Driving this idealizing fantasy is the repression and then projection of sexual and violent impulses onto others. In contemporary liberal popular culture, this process can be seen in the constant depiction of criminals and gangsters who are able to live outside of the law.[70] Many successful television series allow the audience the vicarious pleasure of identifying with someone who has direct access to enjoyment. Similar to the investment in pornography, the idealization of violence relates to the unconscious fantasy of instinctual gratification without social guilt or shame.

My argument then is that in order to make a false distinction between conservatives and traditionalists, Robin creates an imaginary version of a pre-premodern society where people experience their impulses directly through tradition. Similar to a return to the Garden of Eden, this investment in a time before loss, guilt, and shame allows people to imagine that at least someone has direct access to unmediated enjoyment.[71] It is possible that Robin has to posit the mythical traditional period before premodern conservative ideology so that he can equate conservatism with reactionary post-postmodern libertarian Right-wing politics. Thus, he will state that conservative ideology is founded on the desire to recover a lost tradition: "They get wrapped in a narrative of loss—in which the revolutionary or reformist plays a necessary part—and presented in a program of recovery" (23). Instead of seeing conservative ideology as based on the conservation of social hierarchies and traditions, he represents it as a politics of recovery, and this move enables him to equate it with the contemporary backlash culture embodied in the idea of "Making America Great Again."[72] It should be clear that this program for recovery does not have a clear set of values that are being sought; instead, Trump's call for a return to greatness is mostly a reaction to the postmodern Left. After all, he never says when America was great and what period he would like to return to. His desire for recovery is therefore an empty gesture shaped by the fantasy that things must have been better before.

While Trump often likes to represent himself as representing law and order and a return to conservative values, it should be clear that he only makes these gestures to gain and sustain political power. As Robin posits, conservative ideology has had a close relation to social order: "The conservative defends particular orders—hierarchical, often private regimes of rule—on the assumption, in part, that hierarchy is order" (24). Although Trump's call for order is more of a political ploy and a backlash against the disorderly Left, true conservatives desire social order because this type of discipline serves to protect the social hierarchy by keeping the masses in check. Of course, the great ideological trick of the Republican party has been the effort to convince the working class to support the billionaire class, and this process has been made possible in part through a shared hatred for liberals and the Left coupled with the use of racism, sexism, and homophobia to pit the masses against each other.[73] In this weaponizing of premodern prejudices, the desire to return to a previous era before the postmodern social movements for justice is shaped by the retention of offensive rhetoric seeking to put women, minorities, and other oppressed groups back in their place.[74]

Unlike the centrist racist fantasy that idealizes the other's access to unmediated enjoyment, the Right sees the debased others as cheating and stealing enjoyment through acts of violence and unlawful behavior.[75] While the libertarian Right fantasizes about their own access to total freedom and enjoyment, contemporary centrists fantasize that the other is able to escape the restraints of civilization. Moreover, since libertarians are invested in a fundamental fantasy of total freedom and enjoyment, the political correctness of the Left is experienced as a violent threat to personal liberty.[76] Therefore, when Trump attacks the liberal media or the politically correct campus activists, he is seeking to defend access to pleasure beyond any social constraint. Here we re-find Robin's claim that, unlike the conservative, the traditionalist has direct access to the objects of desire.

For Robin, the combination of conservative and libertarian ideology can best be understood through the notion that due to the loss of conservative values in the dominant culture, the only way to return to those values is to promote a counter-revolutionary backlash:

> The conservative not only opposes the left; he also believes that the left has been in the driver's seat since, depending on who's counting, the French Revolution or the Reformation. If he is to preserve what he values, the conservative must declare war against the culture as it is. (26)

The idea here is that conservatives cannot simply fight to conserve their values in a culture that has gotten rid of those values, but as I have shown in my analysis of the premodern discourse of the master, it is unclear if these conservative values and prejudices have actually been lost. It might be more accurate to say that premodern conservative ideology still functions as the underlying structure of society and culture, and while modernity seeks a separation from this discourse, conservatism still has a great deal of influence in the world today. In fact, even if social movements on the Left seek to reverse the hierarchies generated from conservative ideology, this revolutionary reversal is structured by the categories and hierarchies produced by the discourse of the master.

The Anti-Elite Elite

In terms of the relation between the contemporary Right and the old conservative order, the key move is to get the masses to support the social hierarchy on a voluntary basis: in other words, in an effort to combine together the premodern discourse of the master with the modern emphasis on freedom and equality, it is necessary to motivate people to freely choose their subordination.[77] Robin describes this ideological magic trick in the following way:

> the right has grown increasingly aware that any successful defense of the old regime must incorporate the lower orders in some capacity other than as underlings or starstruck fans. The masses must either be able to locate themselves symbolically in the ruling class or be provided with real opportunities to become faux aristocrats in the family, the factory, and the field.
>
> (31)

Through the unconscious processes of idealization and identification, the masses are taught to desire inequality so that they can identify with their idealized masters. One way that this ideology is accomplished is through the use of nationalism as a shared form of idealization: thus even if you are poor or suffering, you are part of a greater power.[78] This nationalism strategy is often coupled with the use of prejudice, sexism, and racism to create social hierarchies so that the disempowered masses can feel empowered in comparison to debased social groups.

However, one strategy for motivating the disempowered to identify with those in power that Robin does not stress is the way that the Right gets the working class to identify with the rich and the powerful through a shared sense of victimhood.[79] Therefore, when wealthy white Christians represent themselves as victims of taxes, government regulations, political correctness, and immigration, they can use their victim status to bond with people who are really being victimized by the economic structure. The reason, then, why someone like Trump spends so much time talking about the politically correct Left and the oppressive mainstream media is that he can represent himself as a victim of the elite establishment, when in reality he is the establishment. Here, we see that instead of simply trying to impose the discourse of the master through real or symbolic violence, the main technique is to hide one's power in order to bond with the disempowered.

Trump also feeds this upside-down populism by portraying himself as real, unscripted, and anti-elite.[80] Just as our popular media now focus on reality-based media, Trump appeals to the masses by signaling that he is not a fake, scripted politician; instead, he is just like them.[81] Moreover, by refusing to be censored by the politically correct Left, he feeds into the libertarian desire to be free from social control. As the primal father who has total freedom and direct access to enjoyment, he also becomes a source of vicarious pleasure.[82] Similar to the way Christian leaders now show off their wealth, the elite have learned that they can best protect their power if they show it off so other people can imagine attaining the same level of freedom and enjoyment.[83] Of course, our current media-saturated culture helps to enable this structure because people have so much access to the representation of others.

Since Robin lacks a model of psychopathology, he is only to describe part of the reason why the rich and powerful have been able to gain the support of the working class:

> One cannot perceive this affinity by focusing on disagreements of policy or contingent statements of practice (states' rights, federalism, and so on); one must look to the underlying arguments, the idioms and metaphors, the deep visions and metaphysical pathos evoked in each disagreement and statement.
>
> (32)

Without psychoanalysis, one is left analyzing deep visions and metaphysical pathos instead of the unconscious mechanisms of identification, idealization, and victimhood. In fact, the pathos of the Right is often generated by the political appropriation of postmodern Left-wing social movement strategies.[84] For example, the fights for women's rights, civil rights, worker's rights, and gay rights all organized around a shared trauma that helped to divide the world between the good, innocent victim and the evil perpetrator.[85] As Freud explained in his analysis of what he called hysterical identification, people often bond over a shared sense of suffering.[86] Freud also added that this suffering can be real or imaginary, but what matters is how suffering is used to manipulate other people. Since the suffering victim is always innocent and pure, and the victim cannot be criticized, aggression towards the other is always justified. Moreover, due to the fact that social movements have to create internal solidarity as they clearly mark the difference between the good us and the evil other, they organize over shared victimhood as they represent their other as the victimizer who must be attacked.[87] The Right has taken this structure and reversed its content, and now you have the people with the most social power acting as if they are the victims of the disempowered.

For Robin, this backlash appropriation of Leftist tactics by the Right is called conservatism, but as I have been arguing, it would be better to equate it with libertarianism since it is founded on the dual process of getting the masses to identify with the elite aggressors as one sees the disadvantaged as the true source of inequality. Without a psychoanalytic understanding of how ideology functions in the world today, Robin is left confusing conservatism with the Right: "Unlike the feudal past, where power was presumed and privilege inherited, the conservative future envisions a world where power is demonstrated and privilege earned" (35). While contemporary centrists rely on the myth of a fair meritocracy to maintain power and to justify inequality, the reactionary Right relies on capitalist competition as the main proving ground for individual value. The idealization of the free market, then, is in actuality an idealization of the competition of isolated individuals who have repressed their awareness of larger social structures shaping our everyday interactions.[88] Since the market is never really free, the ideology of the free market obscures the way we are constrained and shaped through a system of laws, contracts, currencies, and social practices. However, because the Right wants to replace class war with a culture war, it has to hide economic determinism behind a battle over words and representations.

As we shall see in the next chapter, one of the great failures of the contemporary Left is to play into the hands of the Right by also focusing on cultural representations and not on social power and economic class. While it is still vital to counter racism and sexism in society and subjectivity, it is necessary to see how these premodern prejudices are utilized by modern capitalism to rationalized and maintain economic and social inequality.

Notes

1 Samuels, Robert. "Trump and sanders on the couch: Neoliberal populism on the left and the right." *Psychoanalyzing the left and right after Donald Trump*. Palgrave Macmillan, 2016, 61–76.

2 Minkenberg, Michael. "The new right in Germany: The transformation of conservatism and the extreme right." *European Journal of Political Research* 22.1 (1992): 55–81.

3 Pagden, Anthony. *The enlightenment: And why it still matters*. Oxford University Press, 2013.

4 Hunter, James Davison. *American evangelicalism: Conservative religion and the quandary of modernity*. Rutgers University Press, 1983.

5 Gorski, Philip. "Why evangelicals voted for Trump: A critical cultural sociology." *Politics of meaning/meaning of politics*. Palgrave Macmillan, 2019, 165–183.

6 Peek, Charles W., George D. Lowe, and L. Susan Williams. "Gender and God's word: Another look at religious fundamentalism and sexism." *Social Forces* 69.4 (1991): 1205–1221.

7 Harris, Harriet A. *Fundamentalism and evangelicals*. Oxford University Press on Demand, 1998.

8 Vopat, Mark. "Is a Libertarian-Christian an oxymoron?" *International Journal of Religion & Spirituality in Society* 2.2 (2013).

9 Fromm, Erich. *Escape from freedom*. Macmillan, 1994.

10 Rensmann, Lars. *The politics of unreason: The Frankfurt School and the origins of modern antisemitism*. Suny Press, 2017.

11 Lacan, Jacques. *The other side of psychoanalysis*. WW Norton, 2007.

12 Newman, William Lambert, ed. *The politics of Aristotle: With an introduction, two prefactory essays and notes critical and explanatory*. Vol. 3. Clarendon Press, 1902.

13 Bracher, Mark. *Lacan, discourse, and social change: A psychoanalytic cultural criticism*. Cornell University Press, 1993.

14 Cummins, Denise. "Dominance, status, and social hierarchies." *The handbook of evolutionary psychology*. John Wiley & Sons, (2005), 676–697.

15 Althusser, Louis. *On the reproduction of capitalism: Ideology and ideological state apparatuses*. Verso Trade, 2014.

16 Žižek, Slavoj. "Invisible ideology: Political violence between fiction and fantasy." *Journal of Political Ideologies* 1.1 (1996): 15–32.

17 Taylor, Gary. *Castration: An abbreviated history of western manhood*. Psychology Press, 2002.

18 Fink, Bruce. *Lacan on love: An exploration of Lacan's seminar VIII, transference*. John Wiley & Sons, 2017.

19 Rhoades, Gary. "Backlash against 'others'." *International Higher Education* 89 (2017): 2–3.

20 Keckler, Charles, and Mark J. Rozell. "The libertarian right and the religious right." *Perspectives on Political Science* 44.2 (2015): 92–99.

21 Epstein, Cynthia Fuchs. *Deceptive distinctions: Sex, gender, and the social order*. Yale University Press, 1988.

22 Freud, Sigmund. "The dissolution of the Oedipus complex." *The standard edition of the complete psychological works of Sigmund Freud, volume XIX (1923–1925): The ego and the Id and other works.* Eds. James Strachey and Anna Freud. London: Hogarth Press, (1961), 171–180.

23 Freud, Sigmund. "The ego and the id." *The standard edition of the complete psychological works of Sigmund Freud, volume XIX (1923–1925): The ego and the Id and other works*. Eds. James Strachey and Anna Freud. London: Hogarth Press(1961), 1–66.

24 Freud, Sigmund. "The economic problem of masochism." *The standard edition of the complete psychological works of Sigmund Freud, volume XIX (1923–1925): The ego and the Id and other works.* Eds. James Strachey and Anna Freud. London: Hogarth Press (1961), 155–170.

25 Rubin, Gayle. "The traffic in women: Notes on the 'political economy' of sex." *Traffic*. Ed. R. Reiter. New York: Monthly Press. 5: 9: 157-210.
26 Etengoff, Chana, and Tyler G. Lefevor. "Sexual prejudice, sexism, and religion." *Current Opinion in Psychology*, 40 (2020): 45-50.
27 Powell, Brian, and Lala Carr Steelman. "Fundamentalism and sexism: A reanalysis of peek and brown." *Social Forces* 60 (1982): 1154–1158.
28 Smith, Nicholas D. "Plato and Aristotle on the nature of women." *Journal of the History of Philosophy* 21.4 (1983): 467–478.
29 Young-Bruehl, Elisabeth. *The anatomy of prejudices*. Harvard University Press, 1998.
30 Marx, Karl, and Friedrich Engels. *The communist manifesto*. Penguin, 2002.
31 Reiman, Jeffrey H. "The fallacy of libertarian capitalism." *Ethics* 92.1 (1981): 85–95.
32 Inglehart, Ronald F., and Pippa Norris. "Trump, Brexit, and the rise of populism: Economic have-nots and cultural backlash." *Harvard JFK School of Government Faculty Working Papers Series* (2016): 1-52.
33 Whittier, Nancy. "The consequences of social movements for each other." *The Blackwell companion to social movements*. David A. Snow, Sarah A. Soule, and Hanspeter Kriesi, eds. Oxford: Blackwell: (2004), 531–551.
34 Valentino, Nicholas A., Carly Wayne, and Marzia Oceno. "Mobilizing sexism: The interaction of emotion and gender attitudes in the 2016 US presidential election." *Public Opinion Quarterly* 82.S1 (2018): 799–821.
35 Samuels, Robert. "Trump and Sanders on the couch: Neoliberal populism on the left and the right." *Psychoanalyzing the left and right after Donald Trump*. Palgrave Macmillan, 2016, 61–76.
36 Yglesias, Matthew. "What Trump has actually done in his first 3 years." *Vox*, December 2 (2019).
37 D'Antonio, Michael, and Peter Eisner. *The shadow president: The truth about Mike Pence*. Thomas Dunne Books, 2018.
38 Sanders, Steve. "The cultural politics of Dan Quayle and Mike Pence." *Indiana Law Review* 52 (2019): 69.
39 Zizek, Slavoj, and Slavoj Žižek. *Welcome to the desert of the real: Five essays on September 11 and related dates*. Verso Trade, 2013.
40 Falbo, Toni, and James A. Shepperd. "Self-righteousness: Cognitive, power, and religious characteristics." *Journal of Research in Personality* 20.2 (1986): 145–157.
41 Žižek, Slavoj. "The rule of law between obscenity and the right to distress." *Zizek and Law*. Bottomley, A. and Moore, Nathan (2016) Sonorous law II: the refrain. In: de Sutter, L. (ed.) Zizek and Law. Abingdon, UK: Routledge. (2015): 220.
42 Esposito, John L. *Unholy war: Terror in the name of Islam*. Oxford University Press, 2003.
43 Fromm, Erich. *Escape from freedom*. Macmillan, 1994.
44 Freud, Sigmund. *Group psychology and the analysis of the ego*. WW Norton & Company, 1975.
45 Jacobson, Edith. "The 'exceptions': An elaboration of Freud's character study." *The Psychoanalytic Study of the Child* 14.1 (1959): 135–154.

46 Whyte, Glen. "Diffusion of responsibility: Effects on the escalation tendency." *Journal of Applied Psychology* 76.3 (1991): 408.
47 Murray, Kelly, and Joseph W. Ciarrocchi. "The dark side of religion, spirituality and the moral emotions: Shame, guilt, and negative religiosity as markers for life dissatisfaction." *Journal of Pastoral Counseling* 42 (2007): 22–41.
48 Handler, Joel F. "Postmodernism, protest, and the new social movements." *Law & Society Review* 26.4 (1992): 697–731.
49 Cummins, Denise. "Dominance, status, and social hierarchies." *The handbook of evolutionary psychology* (2005), 676–697.
50 Bendroth, Margaret. "Last gasp patriarchy: Women and men in conservative American protestantism." *The Muslim World* 91.1/2 (2001): 45.
51 Cole, Andrew. "What Hegel's master/slave dialectic really means." *Journal of Medieval and Early Modern Studies* 34.3 (2004): 577–610.
52 Sartre, Jean-Paul. *Being and nothingness: An essay in phenomenological ontology*. Citadel Press, 2001.
53 Foucault, Michel. *The order of things*. Routledge, 2005.
54 Perrin, Andrew J., J. Micah Roos, and Gordon W. Gauchat. "From coalition to constraint: Modes of thought in contemporary American conservatism." *Sociological Forum* 29.2 (2014): 285–300.
55 Leege, David C., et al. *The politics of cultural differences: Social change and voter mobilization strategies in the post-new deal period*. Princeton University Press, 2009.
56 Clifton, Brett M. "Romancing the GOP: Assessing the strategies used by the Christian coalition to influence the Republican Party." *Party Politics* 10.5 (2004): 475–498.
57 Layman, Geoffrey C., et al. "Activists and conflict extension in American party politics." *American Political Science Review* (2010) 104.2: 324–346.
58 Lasch, Christopher. *The agony of the American left*. Knopf, 2013.
59 Henrich, Joseph, Steven J. Heine, and Ara Norenzayan. "The weirdest people in the world?" *Behavioral and Brain Sciences* 33.2–3 (2010): 61–83.
60 Gergen, Kenneth J. The Saturated Self. New York: Basic Books, 2007.
61 Bolton, Derek, et al. "Magical thinking in childhood and adolescence: Development and relation to obsessive compulsion." *British Journal of Developmental Psychology* 20.4 (2002): 479–494.
62 Sandel, Michael J. *The tyranny of merit: What's become of the common good?* Allen Lane, 2020.
63 van der Toorn, Jojanneke, et al. "In defense of tradition: Religiosity, conservatism, and opposition to same-sex marriage in North America." *Personality and Social Psychology Bulletin* 43.10 (2017): 1455–1468.
64 Boothby, Richard. *Death and desire (RLE: Lacan): Psychoanalytic theory in Lacan's return to Freud*. Routledge, 2014.
65 Cho, Daniel. "Thanatos and civilization: Lacan, Marcuse, and the death drive." *Policy Futures in Education* 4.1 (2006): 18–30.
66 Foucault, Michel. *The history of sexuality: An introduction*. Vintage, 1990.
67 Freud, Sigmund. *Civilization and its discontents*. Broadview Press, 2015.
68 Samuels, Robert. "Simon Clarke and the politics and psychoanalysis of racism." *Psychoanalysis, Culture & Society* 25.1 (2020): 108–112.

69 Mills, Charles W. *Black rights/white wrongs: The critique of racial liberalism*. Oxford University Press, 2017.
70 Berleant, Arnold. "Reflections on the aesthetics of violence." *Contemporary Aesthetics* (Special Volume 7: "Aesthetics and Terrorism" [2019]),64.
71 Frank, Thomas. *What's the matter with Kansas?: How conservatives won the heart of America*. Picador, 2007.
72 McMillan, Chris. "Make America great again: Ideological fantasy, American exceptionalism and Donald Trump." *Subjectivity* 10.2 (2017): 204–222.
73 Frank, Thomas. *Pity the billionaire: The hard-times swindle and the unlikely comeback of the right*. Macmillan, 2012.
74 Norris, Pippa, and Ronald Inglehart. *Cultural backlash: Trump, Brexit, and authoritarian populism*. Cambridge University Press, 2019.
75 Hook, Derek. "Racism and jouissance: Evaluating the "racism as (the theft of) enjoyment" hypothesis." *Psychoanalysis, Culture & Society* 23.3 (2018): 244–266.
76 Samuels, Robert. "Catharsis: The politics of enjoyment." *Zizek and the rhetorical unconscious*. Palgrave Macmillan, 2020, 7–31.
77 Frank, Thomas, and Matt Weiland, eds. *Commodify your dissent: Salvos from the baffler*. WW Norton & Company, 1997.
78 Žižek, Slavoj. *The sublime object of ideology*. Verso, 1989.
79 Samuels, Robert. "Victim politics: Psychoanalyzing the neoliberal conservative counter-revolution." *Psychoanalyzing the left and right after Donald Trump*. Palgrave Macmillan, 2016, 7–29.
80 Quigley, Jared. "An unlikely populist: Donald Trump and the rhetoric of elite and minority resentment." (2018) *Honors Scholar Theses*. 568. https://opencommons.uconn.edu/srhonors_theses/568.
81 Hart, Roderick P. *Trump and us: What he says and why people listen*. Cambridge University Press, 2020.
82 Foster, Hal. "Père Trump." *October* (2017): 3–6.
83 Bowler, Kate. *Blessed: A history of the American prosperity gospel*. Oxford University Press, 2018.
84 Samuels, Robert. "Pathos, hysteria, and the left." *Zizek and the rhetorical unconscious*. Palgrave Macmillan, 2020, 33–47.
85 Sztompka, Piotr. "The trauma of social change." *Cultural Trauma and Collective Identity, California University Press, Berkeley* 6 (2004): 155–197.
86 Freud, Sigmund. *Group psychology and the analysis of the ego*. WW Norton & Company, 1975.
87 Giesen, B., and S. N. Eisenstadt. *Triumph and trauma*. Routledge, 2015.
88 Aune, James Arnt. *Selling the free market: The rhetoric of economic correctness*. Guilford Press, 2002.

5 The Hysterical Left and the Narcissistic Center

This chapter examines the relations between the psychopathologies of the Left and liberal centrism. In reading closely Robin DiAngelo's *White Fragility*, I will employ psychoanalytic concepts to clarify what is missing in most accounts of contemporary politics.[1] Of special concern will be the narcissistic structure of contemporary liberalism (centrism) as it relates to the political strategies of the Left. I will also seek to distinguish among premodern conservative racism, Right-wing reactionary racism, and the modern suspension of race. However, unlike DiAngelo, I want to retain a space for universality and neutrality in the law and politics in general.[2] While DiAngelo sees universal claims as necessarily a tool of white supremacy, I argue that it is impossible to have global human rights and democratic institutions if we do not affirm the necessary but impossible ideals of equality and impartial justice.[3] Even when it is shown that these ideals are not lived up to, and we see the role played by racism in our criminal justice system, we have to realize that the problem is only detectable because it is being compared to the ideal of equal justice.[4]

The five-part model of ideology I have presented in this book can help us to frame the discussion of DiAngelo's book. Since her main focus is on the ways progressive liberals (centrists) refuse to acknowledge their own racism and white privilege, she tends to take on the position of the Left, and so it is important to recognize this difference between liberals and the Left. She also focuses on the reason why the modern investment in universality, objectivity, and neutrality are actually products of white supremacy as she ties the birth of racism to modernity and not to the premodern period of conservative ideology. This displacement of the origins of racism results in a series of theoretical and practical problems that will be examined here. Related to this lack of historical clarity is her tendency to equate the centrist repression of racism to the Right-wing libertarian

DOI: 10.4324/9781003199649-5

backlash against race-based politics and policies. Once again, these seemingly academic issues have very important real-life consequences, and since she does not have a psychoanalytic understanding of the ideologies she discusses, there is also a tendency to over-generalize and polarize. One of the effects of her discourse is to place her readers in the uncomfortable position of having to admit their guilt and shame, while she retains a position of disavowed moral superiority.

Divisive Rhetoric

The divisive nature of her work starts with her representation of American history as a battle between the ideal of universal legal equality and the reality of violence and inequality:

> The United States was founded on the principle that all people are created equal. Yet the nation began with the attempted genocide of Indigenous people and the theft of their land. American wealth was built on the labor of kidnapped and enslaved Africans and their descendants. Women were denied the right to vote until 1920, and black women were denied access to that right until 1965. The term identity politics refers to the focus on the barriers specific groups face in their struggle for equality. We have yet to achieve our founding principle, but any gains we have made thus far have come through identity politics.
>
> (xiii)

This struggle between the goal of equal justice and the actuality of inequality marks the relation between modern liberalism and the social movements on the Left. From the perspective of modernity, the law has to apply to everyone on an equal basis, and universal human rights have to be protected equally, but as postmodern social activists have stressed, throughout history, particular groups have been excluded from these rights and laws.[5] One role, then, of the Left is to help expand universal human rights, but a problem often arises when instead of fighting for equal justice, a group focuses only on their own identity as it relates to suffering injustices.[6]

It is vital to acknowledge that little progress would be made in the expansion of human rights if it was not for the organization of oppressed people around shared grievances and identities. We thus need these movements, but we also have to realize their limitations and when they can become counter-productive. As we shall see in the analysis of DiAngelo's work, the dialectical relation between the postmodern social movements on the Left and the modern ideal of equality is undermined when the goals of neutrality, universality, and objectivity are dismissed because they are seen as tools of white supremacy.[7] Instead of accepting the idea that these necessary but impossible ideals structure scientific reason and democratic institutions, many postmodern critics posit that there can be no impartial, universal perspective because the concepts of universality and impartiality were invented by white European males, and so they really represent the vested interests of this particular group.[8] However, I have been arguing that science and democratic justice begin with a bias against bias that is enacted through critical introspection, and while these ideals may never be fully attained, they do produce the standards we use to judge both their success and their failure.

The first way that DiAngelo dismisses the modern ideals of neutrality and equality is by highlighting that everyone is biased, and so all of our social institutions must also be biased:

> While implicit bias is always at play because all humans have bias, inequity can occur simply through homogeneity; if I am not aware of the barriers you face, then I won't see them, much less be motivated to remove them. Nor will I be motivated to remove the barriers if they provide an advantage to which I feel entitled.
>
> (xiii)

On one level, I would not disagree with this notion that we all have biases, but on another level, the problem with this perspective is that it does not allow for the effort to suspend bias in social institutions. Just as the psychoanalyst seeks to stop judging the patient so the patient can say whatever comes into his or her mind, we have to realize that the artificial position of neutrality can be pursued if one actively seeks to work against bias and prejudice by creating systems where everyone is treated the same.[9] Fundamentally, if we do not have this goal of equal treatment, then it is hard to see how universal human rights can be promoted.[10]

Instead of pushing for more equality and impartiality, DiAngelo seeks to show how the very idea of universality is a form of white supremacy and racism: "Not naming the groups that face barriers only serves those who already have access; the assumption is that the access enjoyed by the controlling group is universal" (xiv). The problem with this Left-wing perspective is that it does not allow for any solution beyond the recognition of the problem: since DiAngelo wants to equate universality with white supremacy, all she can do is to point to the examples of inequality, injustice, and racism without providing solutions to the conflict.[11] One possible reason for this tendency on the Left is that people identify with the suffering of members belonging to their own group, and they are invested in identifying themselves as victims as they accuse their social others of being evil perpetrators. From a psychoanalytic perspective, the problem with this structure is not that all victimization is imaginary; rather, the issue is the way suffering can turn into a fixated identity blocking change and awareness.[12] Thus, if there was ever a discourse that was in conflict with identity politics, it is clearly psychoanalysis, which is focused on helping people change by giving up their destructive fixations and identifications.[13] While it is essential not to deny the real suffering of people, psychoanalysis looks at how suffering is used unconsciously to attain pleasure, deny responsibility, and project aggression onto others.[14]

Although DiAngelo spends little time examining the underlying psychological structures shaping Left-wing identity politics, she does analyze some of the unconscious processes circulating in liberal centrist ideology:

> Socialized into a deeply internalized sense of superiority that we either are unaware of or can never admit to ourselves, we become highly fragile in conversations about race. We consider a challenge to our racial worldviews as a challenge to our very identities as good, moral people.
>
> (2)

Here we see how white fragility stems from the centrist's desire to maintain a positive self-image by repressing any feelings of guilt and shame that could be generated through recognizing inequality and racism.[15] Since liberal narcissists want to be seen as being good people with good intentions, they do not want to admit their own prejudices and privileges. Moreover, when someone points out to them their failures to be just and good, they often respond with defensive anger.[16] As Lacan highlights, in the structure of narcissism, the subject wants the ideal ego to be recognized by an ideal Other, and when this recognition is not forthcoming, the subject feels empty or attacked since this subject is defined through the eyes of an approving Other.[17] Furthermore, since the ego is formed by identifying with similar others, the liberal narcissist is doubly alienated because this subject is an other for the Other.[18] One reason then why contemporary liberal politicians can come off as being fake is that they are very concerned with being loved and liked by others, and so they end up pretending to be people they are not.[19]

Beyond Individualism and Universality

This effort to maintain an image of being seen by the self and others as good helps to define white fragility for DiAngelo. Moreover, the focus on good intentions and the maintenance of a positive self-image is shown to be in part based on a denial of racism and other prejudices:

> For example, many white participants who lived in white suburban neighborhoods and had no sustained relationships with people of color were absolutely certain that they held no racial prejudice or animosity. Other participants simplistically reduced racism to a matter of nice people versus mean people. Most appeared to believe that racism ended in 1865 with the end of slavery.
>
> (3)

The problem with this analysis is that it does not clearly distinguish among the different ideologies of the Right, centrists, and conservatives: while the premodern conservative discourse of the master helps to structure society through prejudice, racism, and stereotypes, the Right-wing attack on affirmative action is better understood as an attempt to counter the policies caused by the postmodern Left.[20] Likewise, the contemporary centrist denial of race and racism should be separated from the modern democratic goal of acknowledging and then suspending biases. If we do not make these categorical distinctions, then we are left with a confusing set of problems and no clear solution.

Since DiAngelo equates universality and objectivity with racism and white supremacy, it is difficult to know how she can even attempt to communicate with others. After all, the only reason that we try to share our ideas with different people is that we believe they will try to objectively understand what we are intending and how our words relate to reality.[21] Just as science and democracy are based on necessary but impossible ideals, so too communication and education rely on the ideals of reason, objectivity, and universality; to communicate, we have to at least pretend that the meaning of our words can be understood and that our audience will engage in a good-faith effort at processing our ideas in an objective and rational way.[22] Yet, DiAngelo wants to claim that universality and objectivity are simply the tools of white privilege:

> We make sense of perceptions and experiences through our particular cultural lens. This lens is neither universal nor objective, and without it, a person could not function in any human society. But exploring these cultural frameworks can be particularly challenging in Western culture precisely because of two key Western ideologies: individualism and objectivity.
>
> (9)

Her first point is that since our perceptions and understanding are all shaped by culture, it is impossible to have a universal or objective view of the world. On one level, this notion of the cultural framing of thought and perception is correct, but on another level, it is wrong because it does not allow for critical introspection and the application of what Freud called the reality principle.[23] Thus, through critical self-awareness, we can attempt to overcome our cultural and personal biases by first acknowledging and then suspending our prejudices, but this is not a natural or inevitable process. Luckily, modern society has produced many social institutions and structures that help to suspend bias because these systems go beyond the power of separate individuals.[24] Although universities, research institutes, and legal systems can fail to live up to their ideals, they do have the potential of pursuing universality and objectivity, and while these defining principles may not actually exist in a pure state, they do function to structure modern social practices.[25]

Not only does DiAngelo desire to see objectivity as an oppressive tool developed by Western ideology, but she also criticizes the modern conception of individualism. One reason for this critique is that she wants people to see racism as a system and not the result of the actions of isolated individuals.[26] She also desires to convince her audience that our sense of seeing the world as separate individuals is an illusion blocking our ability to understand how our perceptions are framed by cultural influences:

> Individualism is a story line that creates, communicates, reproduces, and reinforces the concept that each of us is a unique individual and that our group memberships, such as race, class, or gender, are irrelevant to our opportunities. Individualism claims that there are no

> intrinsic barriers to individual success and that failure is not a consequence of social structures.
>
> (10)

While it is clear that a problem with contemporary centrist liberalism is that it often focuses on the individual as the locus of perception and power, we also find the same problem in the Right-wing emphasis on individual liberty.[27] From this perspective, both ideologies fail to grasp the power of culture and society to shape us as individuals, but for the Right, the goal is to reduce or eliminate social mediation, whereas, for the liberal centrist, the desire is often to conform to the social system.[28] Moreover, both of these conceptions of individualism block us from seeing that modern liberalism functions by protecting the rights and freedom of each individual by having everyone submit to the same set of rules and norms.[29] The paradox of this structure is that individual freedom is gained through social submission, but unlike the submissive subjectivity required by premodern conservativism, modern liberal democracy seeks to maintain two opposite forces at the same time: the impersonal public law and the personal freedom of the private individual. It is therefore the separation of the public realm from the private realm that is one of the defining aspects of modernity itself.[30]

I have been arguing here that DiAngelo's analysis of how to teach centrist liberals about racism often suffers from its inability to clearly distinguish among different ideological structures, and this conceptual problem also results in the undermining of any possible social solution since the ideals of the solution are themselves criticized and dismissed. DiAngelo not only wants to associate universality, objectivity, and individualism with white racism, but she also rejects efforts to overcome bias through verbal discourse:

> In addition to challenging our sense of ourselves as individuals, tackling group identity also challenges our belief in objectivity. If group membership is relevant, then we don't see the world from the universal human perspective but from the perspective of a particular kind of human.
>
> (11)

As I have been arguing, there can be no science or human rights without universality and objectivity, but like many other Leftist critics and activists, DiAngelo sees these social concepts as the problem and not part of the solution.[31] Since she is focused on how group identities shape our perceptions of the world, she rejects the modern call for an impartial judge of empirical evidence.

In one telling moment, DiAngelo acknowledges that her own discourse can be seen as a contradiction because her criticism of universal generalizations is countered by her tendency to generalize about white people:

> many white people, the mere title of this book will cause resistance because I am breaking a cardinal rule of individualism—I am generalizing. I am proceeding as if I could know anything about someone just because the person is white.
>
> (11)

According to her own definition, DiAngelo does appear to have a racist view of white people, since she does represent them as all being the same, but she also argues that only people without power can be the victims of racism.[32] Yet, this conflict of over-generalizing about one groups' tendency to over-generalize does reveal the way her own discourse relies on the same tools she seeks to reject.[33]

The Leftist Super-Ego

While all human thought requires abstraction and generalization, what defines modernity is the application of empirical reality testing, and this form of the reality principle requires working against passionate attachments and fixed identities.[34] Neutrality, universality, and objectivity are different names for the same process, and when this process is simply dismissed as bias, there is no way to advance the goals of science or democratic law. It therefore becomes important to examine why someone like DiAngelo would seek to expose the social problem of racism but undermine any possible resolution. Is it more important for people on the Left to suffer and be right than to pursue true justice?[35] I believe that only psychoanalysis can help us understand this self-defeating behavior that is centered on making others feel guilty and ashamed for their thoughts and actions, while no real solution is made possible. Part of this psychopathology entails identifying with the super-ego by projecting guilt and shame onto others as one maintains the position of the innocent and pure victim.[36] There is thus a passionate attachment to one's victim identity, and this unconscious attachment blocks advancement.[37]

As Freud discovered in his work with both male and female hysterical patients, they were often fixated on real and imaginary scenes of victimization and suffering.[38] He also noted that suffering can be used to manipulate other people to do what the subject wanted, but this manipulation was often repressed and unconscious.[39] Although Freud's theory can appear to be blaming the victim, what he tried to do was to see how people used their sense of suffering as a way of influencing others. For instance, as we see in many aspects of DiAngelo's Left-wing politics, she wants to employ the suffering of specific minority groups to make white people feel guilt and shame, and by triggering these unconscious affects she seeks to change their behavior.[40] From this perspective, we see how Left-wing social movements often take on the role of the super-ego as they try to fight injustice by activating guilt and censoring words and actions they consider to be immoral or offensive.[41] In turn, Right-wing movements respond to the Leftist super-ego by rallying against censorship or political correctness.[42] As a way of defending their drives and id, the libertarian Right rebels against the censorship of the Left. Furthermore, the activists on the Left seek to deny their own aggression by projecting it onto the Right.[43]

Anti-Reason Reason

In fact, it is notable that when DiAngelo seeks to justify her own use of generalizations, she turns to science to remove herself from any guilt or blame:

> As a sociologist, I am quite comfortable generalizing; social life is patterned and predictable in measurable ways. But I understand that my generalizations may cause some defensiveness for the white people about whom I am generalizing, given how cherished the ideology of individualism is in our culture.
>
> (12)

By pointing to the ways social science measure their generalizations, she indicates that the modern discourse of reason, objectivity, impartiality, and universality is necessary to her project, and yet these are the very conceptual tools she wants to critique and reject. Her discourse has to be thus considered to be ironic and contradictory since it is divided against itself. Here we encounter the ways that progressive academic discourse sometimes attempts to combine conformity to modern science with an investment in Left-wing activism.[44] Since the ideology of social movements requires a biased perspective through the affirmation of fixated identities and identifications, it is at odds with the modern scientific need to be objective, neutral, universal, and empirical.

The main way that DiAngelo seeks to avoid recognizing the contradictions of her own discourse is to make a universal claim about racism: "None of these situations exempts you from the forces of racism, because no aspect of society is outside of these forces" (13). In insisting that there is no escape from racism, she refuses to accept the modern fight against bias as she both blames and absolves her own bias; since everyone and everything is racist, then no one is really responsible, and there is no way beyond this problem. From a psychoanalytic perspective, the theory of hysteria helps us understand how the use of exaggeration and emotional hyperbole functions to remove any sense of proportion as one imagines a world of extreme oppositions.[45]

Moreover, what tilts her project to the hysterical Left is that instead of seeking to recognize and reject discrimination, she strives to make others feel guilt and shame for a system she has represented as being inevitable: "The racial status quo is comfortable for white people, and we will not move forward in race relations if we remain comfortable. The key to moving forward is what we do with our discomfort" (14). She wants people to feel uncomfortable because she wants them to feel guilt and shame, and while this awareness may be a step in the right direction, it is only part of the solution if it is also pointed to a transformation that breaks with fixated identity and emotion. Without this second step, the presentation of racism and suffering caused by oppression ends up being used to manipulate others by making them feel ashamed and guilty for their role in discrimination.[46] Furthermore, as DiAngelo illustrates, centrist liberals want to escape feelings of guilt and shame related to accusations of racism, and so they repress their awareness of how they are part of the problem. None of these ideological responses lead to overcoming the problem because they are all centered on their own defense mechanisms.

It is my hope that part of the solution is for us to have a greater understanding of the unconscious processes shaping our ideological psychopathologies. This mode of education has to be coupled with an increased awareness of how our modern institutions of science and democracy can function by producing social practices centered on reason, universality, and reality testing.[47] However, this call for empiricism is often blocked by the way ideologies function through group processes centered on identification and the suspension of the reality principle.[48] On the level of the hysterical group identity and identification, it is necessary to imitate the ideas and actions of others in order to build group solidarity, and one of the results of this process is often the submission to the impulses of others. As Freud articulated in his analysis of the state of being in love and hypnosis, the follower is often blind to the irrationality and immorality of the Other, and so just as the lover can become blind to the faults of the beloved, the follower of a political movement can give up the ability to judge the truth and morality of the movement itself.[49]

Political Splitting

One of the main ideological tactics that we find in social movements on the Left and the Right is the process of splitting where a clear opposition is formed between two extremes. In DiAngelo's discourse, this type of polarization is presented in the following statement:

> Every aspect of being white discussed in this chapter is shared by virtually all white people in the Western context generally and the US context specifically. At the same time, no person of color in this context can make these same claims.
>
> (51)

According to this binary logic, only white people can have power and privilege, and people of color are by definition excluded from these social attributes.[50] It should be evident that this is an absurd and exaggerated claim, but it does serve the purpose of creating a clear split between the evil perpetrators and the good victims, and since the victims can never be criticized, all of the blame and shame is projected onto the evil Other. In this hysterical structure, not only is the in-group projected against being examined critically by people outside of the group, but the in-group also protects itself against inner criticism, and therefore the modern process of critical introspection is suspended.[51]

As we have seen, there is also a tendency in these polarized groups to create a hysterical sense of pathos and extreme emotion through the rhetoric of hyperbole.[52] In DiAngelo's case, a key way that she seeks to manipulate the emotions of her audience is by using the term "white supremacy" to describe both actual white supremacists (Nazis, Klan members, Neo-fascists) and modern social practices that seek to deny or suspend considerations of race.[53] Due to the lack of proportion in equating people who want a colorblind society and real white supremacists,

DiAngelo tends to efface important historical differences: "I am often asked if I think the younger generation is less racist. No, I don't. In some ways, racism's adaptations over time are more sinister than concrete rules such as Jim Crow" (50). There should be a clear difference between the institution of segregation enforced by the law and current forms of racism, but in order to make an extreme argument, DiAngelo has to efface historical differences and signs of social progress.[54] We see here an underlying fatalism to her discourse, and this fatalism feeds into a premodern conservative ideology, which insists that we are fated to submit to our social positions.[55]

Psychoanalyzing Society

If psychoanalysis has taught us anything, it is that we can rarely get people to change by making them feel guilty or ashamed. Through the process of free association, people have to discover on their own, their faults and conflicts, and then they have to want to change them.[56] However, if we want to make society less racist or structured by bias, we cannot simply require everyone to undertake long psychoanalysis, so we must ask how can we use psychoanalysis on a social level? The first part of the solution is to help people to understand the underlying unconscious processes shaping their thoughts and their actions, but this effort will only take us so far. The next stage that I have been promoting is to clarify the values and principles shaping modern democratic and scientific practices. One reason why this type of education is necessary is that we need to understand how modern liberal institutions and practices work and what differentiates them from other ideological structures. We also need to spread these modern ideals to other aspects of our personal and social lives, and so it is essential to comprehend what values they represent.[57]

I believe that one reason we are seeing a political backlash against modern institutions is that we have failed to teach people about the moral principles underlying modernity itself. Since we do not understand the value of the necessary but impossible ideals of universality and neutrality, we are prone to dismiss them or react against them. Even Leftists like DiAngelo show a strong tendency to attack the very values that make her discourse possible. Since she sees universality and objectivity as tools of white supremacy, she is unable to provide an effective counter to racism. To help correct this problem, I will turn to Anthony Pagden's *The Enlightenment: Why It Matters Now* in order to further define the modern ideology of universal reason.

Notes

1 DiAngelo, Robin. *White fragility: Why it's so hard for white people to talk about racism*. Beacon Press, 2018.
2 Wrange, Pål. "Impartial or uninvolved? The anatomy of 20th century doctrine on the law of neutrality." *The anatomy of 20th century doctrine on the law of neutrality.* Vallingby: Elanders, 2007.
3 Samuels, Robert. "Logos, global justice, and the reality principle." *Zizek and the rhetorical unconscious*. Palgrave Macmillan, 2020, 65–86.
4 Rakowski, Eric. *Equal justice*. Clarendon Paperbacks, 1991.
5 Unger, Roberto Mangabeira. "The critical legal studies movement." *Harvard Law Review*, 96 (1983): 561–675.
6 Alcoff, Linda Martín, and Satya P. Mohanty. "Reconsidering identity politics: An introduction." *Identity politics reconsidered.* Palgrave Macmillan, 2006, 1–9.
7 Samuels, Robert. *Teaching writing, rhetoric, and reason at the Globalizing University*. Routledge, 2020.
8 Inoue, Asao B. *Antiracist writing assessment ecologies: Teaching and assessing writing for a socially just future*. WAC Clearinghouse, 2015.
9 Portuges, Stephen. "The politics of psychoanalytic neutrality." *International Journal of Applied Psychoanalytic Studies* 6.1 (2009): 61–73.
10 Donnelly, Jack. *Universal human rights in theory and practice*. Cornell University Press, 2013.
11 Minow, Martha. "Beyond universality." *University of Chicago Legal Forum* (1989): 115.
12 Arlow, Jacob A. "Unconscious fantasy and disturbances of conscious experience." *The Psychoanalytic Quarterly* 38.1 (1969): 1–27.
13 Nicol, Bran. "As if: Traversing the fantasy in Žižek." *Paragraph* 24.2 (2001): 140–155.
14 Lacan, Jacques. "Intervention on transference." *In Dora's case: Freud—Hysteria—Feminism*. Eds. C. Bernheimer. London: Virago, 1985, 92–104.
15 Samuels, Robert. "Transference and narcissism." *Freud for the twenty-first century*. Palgrave Pivot, 2019, 43–51.
16 Miller, Joshua D., W. Keith Campbell, and Paul A. Pilkonis. "Narcissistic personality disorder: Relations with distress and functional impairment." *Comprehensive Psychiatry* 48.2 (2007): 170–177.
17 Lacan, Jacques. "Remarque sur le rapport de Daniel Lagache: "Psychanalyse et structure de la personnalité." *Écrits.* Edited by Jacques-Alain-Miller. Paris: Le Seuil. (1966): 647–684.
18 Lacan, Jacques. "The mirror stage as formative of the function of the I as revealed in psychoanalytic experience." *Cultural Theory and Popular Culture. A Reader*. New York: Pearson, 2006: 287–292.
19 Lander, Christian. *Stuff white people like: A definitive guide to the unique taste of millions*. Random House, 2008.
20 Rensmann, Lars. *The politics of unreason: The Frankfurt School and the origins of modern antisemitism*. Suny Press, 2017.
21 Habermas, Jurgen, Axel Honneth, and Hans Joas. *Communicative action*. Vol. 1. MIT Press, 1991.

22 Moscovici, Serge. "Social representations and pragmatic communication." *Social Science Information* 33.2 (1994): 163–177.
23 Samuels, Robert. "Science and the reality principle." *Freud for the twenty-first century*. Palgrave Pivot, 2019, 5–16.
24 Henrich, Joseph. *The WEIRDest people in the world: How the west became psychologically peculiar and particularly prosperous*. Farrar, Straus and Giroux, 2020.
25 Readings, Bill. *The university in ruins*. Harvard University Press, 1996.
26 Feagin, Joe. *Systemic racism: A theory of oppression*. Routledge, 2013.
27 Barry, Norman. *On classical liberalism and libertarianism*. Springer, 1987.
28 Bunge, Mario. "Ten modes of individualism—none of which works—and their alternatives." *Philosophy of the Social Sciences* 30.3 (2000): 384–406.
29 Brennan Jr, William J. "State constitutions and the protection of individual rights." *Harvard Law Review* 90 (1976): 489.
30 Bauman, Zygmunt. *Liquid modernity*. John Wiley & Sons, 2013.
31 Chatterjee, Partha. *Our modernity*. No. 1. Rotterdam: Sephis, 1997.
32 Goldberg, David Theo. *Anatomy of racism*. University of Minnesota Press, 1990.
33 Chambless, Dianne L. "Beware the dodo bird: The dangers of overgeneralization." *Clinical Psychology: Science and Practice* 9.1 (2002): 13–16.
34 Hunt, Shelby D. "A realist theory of empirical testing resolving the theory-ladenness/objectivity debate." *Philosophy of the Social Sciences* 24.2 (1994): 133–158.
35 Fraser, Nancy. "Social justice in the age of identity politics." In *Geographic thought: A praxis perspective.* Ed. George Henderson. London: Routledge. (2009), 72–91.
36 Leys, Ruth. *From guilt to shame: Auschwitz and after*. Princeton University Press, 2009.
37 Stone, Lawrence. "Passionate attachments in the west in historical perspective." *Passionate attachments: Thinking about love.* New York: Free Press,1988, 15–27.
38 Menaker, Esther. "The masochistic factor in the psychoanalytic situation." *The Psychoanalytic Quarterly* 11.2 (1942): 171–186.
39 Freud, Sigmund. *Dora: An analysis of a case of hysteria*. Simon and Schuster, 1997.
40 Ellison, Julie. "A short history of liberal guilt." *Critical Inquiry* 22.2 (1996): 344–371.
41 Levitt, Cyril. "Roots of radicalism: Jews, Christians, and the *new left.*" *The Canadian Journal of Sociology.* Summer 1984: 350–357.
42 D'souza, Dinesh. *Illiberal education: The politics of race and sex on campus*. Simon and Schuster, 1991.
43 Robins, Robert Sidwar Robins, Robert S. Robins, and Jerrold M. Post. *Political paranoia: The psychopolitics of hatred*. Yale University Press, 1997.
44 Lindblom, Charles Edward, and David K. Cohen. *Usable knowledge: Social science and social problem solving*. Vol. 21. Yale University Press, 1979.
45 Burt, Andrew. *American hysteria: The untold story of mass political extremism in the United States*. Rowman & Littlefield, 2015.

46 Snyder, Jack. "Backlash against naming and shaming: The politics of status and emotion." *The British Journal of Politics and International Relations* 22.4 (2020): 644–653.
47 Samuels, Richard, Stephen Stich, and Luc Faucher. "Reason and rationality." *Handbook of epistemology*. Springer, 2004, 131–179.
48 Freud, Sigmund. *Group psychology and the analysis of the ego*. WW Norton & Company, 1975.
49 Holowchak, M. Andrew. *Freud: From individual psychology to group psychology*. Jason Aronson, Incorporated, 2012.
50 Brunner, José. *Freud and the politics of psychoanalysis*. Routledge, 2018.
51 Carser, Diane. "The defense mechanism of splitting: Developmental origins, effects on staff, recommendations for nursing care." *Journal of Psychosocial Nursing and Mental Health Services* 17.3 (1979): 21–28.
52 Samuels, Robert. "Pathos, hysteria, and the left." *Zizek and the rhetorical unconscious*. Palgrave Macmillan, 2020, 33–47.
53 Gillborn, David. "Rethinking white supremacy: Who counts in 'WhiteWorld'." *Ethnicities* 6.3 (2006): 318–340.
54 Ray, Victor, and Louise Seamster. "Rethinking racial progress: a response to Wimmer." *Ethnic and Racial Studies* 39.8 (2016): 1361–1369.
55 Gregersen, Niels H. "Theology and disaster studies: From 'acts of God' to divine presence." *Disaster research*. Routledge, 2015, 48–62.
56 Kris, Anton O. *Free association: Methods and process*. Routledge, 2013.
57 Samuels, Robert. "Science and the reality principle." *Freud for the twenty-first century*. Palgrave Pivot, 2019, 5–16.

6 The Anti-Ideology Ideology

Re-Discovering the Enlightenment

A central argument of this book is that we need to understand the psychopathologies of liberal, Left-wing, Right-wing, conservative, and centrist ideologies as we affirm that the alternative to these social and subjective structures derives from the modern conceptions of liberalism, universality, neutrality, and empiricism in science and law. To help clarify what I mean by modern liberalism, I will read closely Anthony Pagden's *The Enlightenment*.[1] I turn to this work because it is my belief that we are currently witnessing a global political backlash against modernity, and part of this reactionary politics is derived from a fundamental misunderstanding of how the philosophy of the Enlightenment helped to shape essential social institutions that still structure our world today.[2] I will provide a psychoanalytic understanding of modern reason to explore some of the more hidden and complicated aspects of this cultural perspective.

Defining Reason

On the most basic level, Pagden defines the Enlightenment by the notion that universal reason can make society more equal and just. As a way of overcoming the premodern reliance on faith, fate, prejudice, and social hierarchy, the modern investment in universal reason is positioned to free humans from their submission to a predetermined social order.[3] Thus, according to the early modern thinker Condorcet, the end result of this ongoing process of enlightenment and liberation will be a world without prejudice and inequality: "All peoples should one day approach the state of civilization attained by the most enlightened, the most free, and the most free from prejudices, such as are the French and the Anglo-Americans." It is important to stress that the desire for a more perfect form of civilization required overcoming prejudice and the previous forms of social inequality.[4] Of course, this move towards perfection

DOI: 10.4324/9781003199649-6

could only be a continual work in progress, but what is important is that our actions are guided by the necessary but impossible ideals of equality, freedom, and universality. In fact, I believe that universality is another word for equality and globalization, and from this perspective, modern liberalism is the ideology of a globalized world.[5]

As Pagden himself points out, people have become critical of the Enlightenment and modern liberalism because they see its globalizing forces as eliminating cultural and individual differences: "Condorcet understood it not as some undifferentiated cultural and political state that all peoples should be compelled to adopt but what he called an 'equal diffusion of enlightenment'" (3). The central idea here is that modern universality does not make everyone the same; instead, it seeks to give everyone the same mental tools so that they can use reason to understand the world around them.[6] While this quest for a more educated and reasonable global civilization may seem overly optimistic, the actual truth is that we are witnessing a constant increase in all of the global indicators of progress.[7] Not only are people living longer, but they are more educated, and they have never had more rights protected. While the Right-wing and Left-wing reactions to globalization get most of the attention, the reality is that on the whole, religion is dying out, and the number of people who base their life decisions on science and not superstition continues to grow.[8] As people become healthier, wealthier, and more literate, they turn away from premodern belief systems, and this transformation often occurs without revolution or even the awareness of most people.

One of the strangest things about our global progress is that people think we are actually regressing, and few people understand what is really happening. This lack of awareness introduces a philosophical problem since we have been taught by the Enlightenment itself that social progress is driven by conscious knowledge. The question then is how has modern reason been able to restructure the world when most people appear to be ignorant of this process? The central answer is that progress has been maintained by social institutions and practices that transcend the consciousness of individual people. In other words, we have created shared systems that can function without most people understanding how they work.[9] The next question is if these social formations get the job done without our awareness, why do we need to learn about them, and the two main answers are that we have to defend these structures against countering forces, and we have to continue to build new structures that are shaped by these ideals. The understanding of the ideology of modern liberalism is thus essential to both of these tasks, and this need to understand and defend modernity is the driving motivation behind this book.[10]

Beyond Religion

While many early modern thinkers believed that we should take on religion directly in order to clear a space for science, reason, and democracy, others have insisted on separating religion from the state in a form of a permanent cease-fire.[11] Not only has the latter option proved to be more peaceful, but it also has functioned to allow for progress to occur in a more subtle and unconscious manner. However, there were some early modern thinkers like Condorcet who did insist that only a direct confrontation between modernity and premodern religion could enable reason to flourish (4). For Condorcet, religion had to be overcome because it kept people in slavery and ignorance, and so the only way to allow people to be free and rational was to reject the illusions generated by premodern magical thinking.[12] However, in reality, modernity has extended its influence not predominantly by a violent confrontation with the premodern but through the very tools of modernity itself: reason, universality, individual freedom, and critical introspection.

However, as Pagden points out, the more modernity actually succeeds in shaping our world, the more people seem to not believe in its ideals or achievements (5). One reason why the success of the modern Enlightenment has been repressed is that as we develop more international democratic institutions, we also see a rise of reactionary nationalism, and the increased visibility of the Right-wing backlash gets most of the media attention.[13] Part of the cause of this problem is that the media feed off of immediate negative stories, and they have a hard time discussing slow global progress.[14] Moreover, humans have a tendency to take progress for granted as they quickly adjust to the new normal.[15] For example, many women in college say that they dislike feminism, but they would not be in school if it was not for the previous women's rights social movement.[16]

Since we are blind to global progress and the ideals that shape our world, we are unable to believe that we can fix problems like climate change or dire poverty. However, the only way that we will gain confidence in our ability to overcome huge global problems is if we recognize what we have done successfully in the past. It is therefore essential to understand the history and philosophy of global progress, and here we see why the humanities still matter in education.[17] If we do not study our history or the ideas shaping our history, we will be blind to ourselves and the world around us. As Pagden insists, the Enlightenment was an age of philosophy, and this type of philosophical thinking was grounded on the combination of doubt and shared logic: "It was a period that sought to overturn every intellectual assumption, every dogma, every 'prejudice' (a favorite term) that had previously exercised any hold over the minds of men" (11). As Kant argues, a key aspect of reason is that it must be held to public criticism; thus, any idea or belief should be open to public scrutiny, and this definition of reason makes it both social and undogmatic.[18] Not only must one learn to critique the ideas of others, but one has to critique one's own ideas, and here we see how Freud's theory of the reality principle comes into play.

Freud and Neutrality

Freud thought that because people are so driven by the pleasure principle to avoid all tension and conflict, it is not natural or inevitable for people to accept the reality of their lives.[19] Since our minds can transcend reality, we are prone to magical thinking, and we have a hard time differentiating between our desires and actuality.[20] Moreover, humans are prone to submit to the ideas of others, and so they are often ignorant of their own beliefs. It is thus a challenge for people to use reason and test reality, but they need to learn how to separate their own self-interest and bias from how they see themselves and the world around them, and the main way this type of advancement occurs is through a slow process of mourning and disinvesting in previous thoughts and feelings.[21] Furthermore, the analytic process helps motivate this process by creating an artificial relationship where the analyst refuses to judge the patient, and the patient learns how to speak without judging himself or herself.

The psychoanalytic notions of analytic neutrality and free association dovetail with the modern ideal of critical introspection and scientific and democratic impartiality.[22] Since these are human ideals constructed out of social negotiation, they do not occur naturally through the process of natural selection. As a practice of the Enlightenment, psychoanalysis begins with Freud's own self-analysis in his *Interpretation of Dreams*, and yet Freud's own work was limited by the fact that he was not analyzed by someone else.[23] The reason why every psychoanalyst needs to be analyzed is that not only does the analyst have to become aware of his or her own prejudices and biases, but it is necessary to work through how we transfer responsibility onto other people and entities.[24] Just as the scientist or politician needs to be open to public scrutiny, the psychoanalyst has to be analyzed by another person, but this person cannot act as the one who knows because one can only discover one's truth through experience.[25]

Global Institutions

In terms of contemporary politics and ideology, modern liberalism requires a self-critical global perspective based on reason and universal human rights, and yet currently we see little evidence of this type of politics.[26] After all, there is no global party, and even politicians in global institutions, like the United Nations, tend to be centered on national perspectives; however, if we want to deal with global issues like pandemics and climate change, then we have to realize that all politics is global now, and so we have to move beyond the limits of the nation-state.[27] In fact, we are seeing an increase in international organizations, but we still do not have a politics to match this globalizing process.

For many people, globalization is still equated with the spread of multinational corporations, and this economic version of universality is often seen in a negative light because any and every social problem can be blamed on this amorphous, all-encompassing system.[28] While I do not want to deny many of the negative effects of contemporary global capitalism, it is also important to realize that the average global standard of living has never been higher, and more people have been lifted out of the dire period in the last 50 years (1970–2020) than in the entire history of humankind.[29] Unfortunately, this important history is repressed behind the focus on the concentration of wealth and disruptive events like the COVID-19 pandemic, and so most people do not know the positive aspects of global capitalism. From the perspective of modernity, capitalism is a necessary social institution because it allows for an increase in social and geographical mobility and interdependence.[30] As Marx himself insisted, modern capitalism melts away all traditional beliefs and structures as it spreads around the world connecting diverse people together.[31] Since the three main social institutions of modernity are science, democracy, and capitalism, it is important to understand how they relate to each other and what they share in common. However, many academic historians and politicians have a Left-wing ideological response to global capitalism, and so they have limited our comprehension to this vital issue.[32]

Modern Ideology

Returning to Pagden's historical account of the Enlightenment, we see that he tends to separate discussion of modern capitalism from his analysis of science and democracy, but what connects all three of these modern institutions is that according to Condorcet, they offer an alternative to the premodern way of seeing the world: "they possess a truth which was independent of the dogmas of religion, of fundamentals, and of sects." While modern thinkers sought to replace religious dogma and prejudice with a new morality based on reason and critical self-analysis, they ran into the problem of how to build an ideology that was itself anti-ideological. Thus, even if we say that science is grounded on the bias against bias, this principle is itself a type of bias, and so there is no way of completely escaping from the realm of ideology.[33] The question then becomes what ideology is best for all of humankind.

A paradox of modern ideology, then, is that it wants to produce a shared social order, but it also needs to provide freedom of thought to individuals. The solution to this problem is centered on a dialectical process where critical introspection is coupled with social institutions that are themselves open to scrutiny and continual revision.[34] In fact, the most apparent aspect of this modern dialectic is evident in the way modern liberalism counters premodern conservative ideology:

> For MacIntyre, all that the Enlightenment project had aimed at was the application of the rational intellect to the murky reaches of the human mind, wherein lurked the menacing, disruptive forces of prejudice, religion, superstition, uncontrolled and unimagined emotions, everything that conspired to deprive the autonomous individual of self-knowledge and self-control.
>
> (11)

Since the only way to have public institutions that are non-dogmatic is to make sure that they are open to criticism, this is only possible if people are provided with rights protecting their freedom of speech and thought.[35] Moreover, if we want people to be able to judge these institutions, we have to educate them and motivate them to use reason and not magical thinking. Many of the world's democratic institutions are based on this logic, but it is clearly a work in progress to get people to use reason to fairly and accurately judge themselves and their social institutions.

From this perspective, education and parenting are essential in training democratic citizens, but due to its commitment to individual freedom, a democracy cannot tell its people how to raise their children or what to teach their students.[36] Therefore, an essential conflict of modernity is the need to allow for both individual freedom and rational social organization at the same time. From a psychoanalytic perspective, this conflict can never be resolved, and the real problem occurs when we attempt to repress it or solve it on an imaginary level. Since we will never transcend the fundamental conflict between society and the individual, we have to learn how to acknowledge it and accept it.[37] This process requires also accepting complexity, ambiguity, and ambivalence, which goes against the pleasure principle's drive to escape any tension or conflict. In fact, for psychoanalysis, anxiety is a necessary sign of the inescapable conflicts shaping human existence, but that does not mean that we should give up trying to make our world more just and understandable.[38] As Pagden insists, the key to the Enlightenment is the role played by continual doubt, which should fuel our desire to improve by never accepting anything without scrutiny (12). From this perspective, education should not be about memorizing facts and information; rather, education should be focused on critical analysis, and nothing should be protected from public scrutiny.[39]

In contrast to this promotion of modern reason, a problem with the current Left-wing ideology is that it often seeks to shut down discussions of issues because they may offend someone, but if we want to pursue liberal globalism, then we have to make sure that any and every idea can come into question.[40] From this perspective, identity and identity politics have to be suspended so that truth can be discovered, but this does not mean that everyone is entitled to their own facts or that educators should spend time discussing opinions.[41] The solution to this contemporary educational problem is to concentrate on the analysis of facts and the methodologies used to examine those facts. Moreover, instead of engaging in opinions and political beliefs, students should study how opinions and ideologies are constructed and maintained. As I have argued throughout this book, his process requires using the concepts of psychoanalysis to clarify the unconscious processes shaping our beliefs and emotional responses.[42] However, what we are currently seeing is the attempt to base human thought on inherited mental programs, and this ideology not only robs us of our freedom, but it also blocks us from seeing the role culture and subjectivity play in constructing social institutions.[43]

The Morality of Modern Science

From a conservative perspective, what is wrong with the modern liberal world view is the focus on science (12). Since conservatives do not see how modern science and democracy have their own moral virtues and principles, they argue that a world based on modernity will be void of any ethical judgments.[44] Yet, as I have been arguing, modern ideology is structured by the principles of equality, empiricism, autonomy, and impartiality, and these ideals are moral virtues, but the problem is that we rarely teach these ideals from the perspective of ethics.[45]

Since few people understand the meaning and the effects of modern liberalism, this ideology is often rejected and attacked for its lack of meaning or morality:

> What had once been looked upon as a means to liberty was now described as a form of enslavement; what had once sought to expose intellectual confusion and the deceptions perpetrated by religion and the uncritical adherence to custom was now seen as itself a form of deception.
>
> (12)

From the perspective of many conservatives and Right-wing reactionaries, the modern world is a soulless place void of meaning and purpose, but these ideological views must be seen as predicated on a radical misunderstanding of modernity itself.[46] Since modern institutions are often able to function effectively with few people understanding what they are or how they work, they are easily attacked and dismissed. In fact, most of the criticisms of modern reason use modern reason to make their arguments, and here they reveal the power of the very discourse they seek to reject. Since we would not even try to communicate with others if we did not think that they were capable of reason, the very act of writing to a public implies an endorsement of modern values and processes.[47] Likewise, if we assume that everyone will interpret whatever we say based on their own prejudices and magical thinking, then we would have no reason to say anything at all. Underlying modernity, thus, is a commitment to the principles of social communication, and once a person tries to be understood by others, one is living under the logic of modern rationality.

Even if we misunderstand each other, and we do not even fully understand ourselves, we cannot help but play by the ideals of reason when we communicate with other people. In a process of pragmatic idealism, we assume that our words relate to a shared reality and that our intended meanings will be understood by ourselves and others, and through a process of approximation and trial and error, we manage to make things happen in the world through our communications.[48] This process is never perfect or complete, but it often gets the job done, and just like the ideals shaping modernity are necessary but impossible, our social interactions require an unstated belief in pragmatic idealism. Not only do we expect others to rationally process our words in good faith, but we also open our own discourse up to the possibility of criticism whether we like it or not. As psychoanalysis teaches us, behind every request to another person, there is a fundamental demand for unconditional recognition, love, and understanding, but there is also an awareness that any demand can be rejected.[49] Modernity takes this conception of communication and uses it to structure our social institutions so that our social worlds can be open to scientific understanding and equal justice.

Rejecting Modernity

Since very few people understand the values and principles supporting our social structures, they often reject the systems that make our lives possible. One form of this rejection has been to tie the Enlightenment to every historical tragedy that has happened during the modern period:

> any belief in any species of universalism could only lead down the road that Europe itself had supposedly traveled, from the delusions of Enlightenment to nationalism, imperialism, and pseudo-scientific racism to the mass mobilization of "scientific socialism" and finally, inexorably, to the gas chambers of Auschwitz.
>
> (13)

The main problem with this common criticism of modernity is that it fails to distinguish between the Enlightenment and the reactions to this philosophy.[50] Since modern liberalism is an ideology promoting universal human rights, it is hard to connect it to imperialism, fascism, or Stalinism.[51] These political ideologies are most often a reaction to modern and postmodern calls for justice and equality; the post-postmodern Right-wing ideology then should be seen as a direct response to postmodern social movements for minority rights.[52] However, many ideologues on the Left seek to reject global modern liberalism because they see it as a fake form of equality that only protects special groups and often serves to promote imperial expansion, totalitarian thinking, and the rejection of premodern cultures.[53]

As Pagden points out, one critique of modernity that continues to circulate today is the Romantic argument that a society based on reason alone is a society without any values or morality:

> All the intellectual revolutions of the nineteenth century, to which the Romantics themselves had unwittingly contributed, the rise of nationalism, the collapse of the human sciences created by "the inflexible Encyclopedists" into Positivism and racism—that "self-assertion of

> the bourgeois individual integrated within a barbaric collective"—and finally neo-Darwinism, eugenics, and the like; all of these and many more were, in Horkheimer and Adorno's view, but the inevitable outcome of the eighteenth-century bid to live by reason alone.
>
> (14)

In response to this effort to equate modern reason with totalitarianism, I have focused on the way that the Enlightenment offers a counter to a premodern order based on social hierarchy, prejudice, and authoritarianism. From this perspective, when modern nations seek to exert their will on others, they are combining modern science and knowledge with premodern ideology.[54] In other words, it is the failure of modernity to achieve its own ideals that pushes leaders and followers to return to a system of strict social inequality. Moreover, I have stressed that there is a morality to modern science, and this involves the necessary but impossible ideals of equality, impartiality, and empiricism. Although some on the Left would like to connect modern capitalism to the invention of racism and slavery, it should be clear that these social formations are derived from premodern ideology.[55]

As Pagden highlights, another criticism by the Left of modernity is that science and reason lead to dehumanization and the treatment of others as merely objects to be calculated and used:

> Postcolonialists and the more radical opponents of "globalization" have cast the Enlightenment, as Adorno and Horkheimer cast it, as the apotheosis of a rationalism that scorns difference and, in the name of science, devastates the environment; strips indigenous peoples of their moral dignity, legal rights, and if possible their cultural identities; and condemns more than two-thirds of the population of the world to penury and misery in order to supply the excessive wants of the other third.
>
> (15)

As Pinker shows, a major problem with this criticism is that it is the combination of modern science, capitalism, and democracy that has helped to bring billions of people out of dire poverty, and while climate change does threaten our existence, there is no way to counter this problem if we do not turn to science itself.[56] While the Left is correct in pointing to wealth inequality as a major global issue, it is vital to focus on the eradication of global poverty instead of simply demonizing the rich.[57] Furthermore, globalization does produce a conflict between premodern cultures and modern science and democracy, but it should be clear that we are moving away from premodern systems structured by social hierarchy, prejudice, faith, fate, and religious authority.[58] It is simply an empirical fact that fewer people are defining their lives through religion, and as the world becomes more globalized, local prejudices and discriminations are reduced. One problem is that we tend to focus on the failures of global modernity and not its successes.

My argument is not that we should simply ignore the real social and subjective issues in the world today, but we need to put them in a long-term global perspective so that we can detect important trends, and many of these trends move in the direction of increased health, wealth, literacy, and human rights. Yet, from the ideology of the Left, global progress is often equated with Western imperialism:

> Empires may be no more, but the universal spirit of the Enlightenment that had made those of the nineteenth century so successful did not vanish with them. It merely changed its language. Enlightenment supposes, in the words of the English philosopher John Gray, a "universal emancipation and a universal civilization." But in reality, this is merely another name for "western cultural imperialism."
>
> (15)

Pagden presents here the typical Left-wing criticism of Enlightenment universality and globalization; instead of realizing the incredible progress that has been made in the world over the last two hundred years, Left-wing ideology is often predicated on taking on a victim-based perspective where capitalism and other global institutions are seen as evil perpetrators bent on hiding their destruction under a veil of good intentions.[59] Although I have been also critical of the way liberal centrists often promote their good intentions, while they hide the negative effects of their actions, the Leftist critique of globalization and the Enlightenment is predicated on a repression of empirical evidence indicating global progress. Not only have we never had fewer wars in the world, but the extension of human lifespans must be seen as an indication that something is working.[60]

Just as we are seeing a global Right-wing backlash against democracy and democratic institutions, we also find in many Left-wing criticisms a similar turn against the Enlightenment institutions of science, capitalism, and democracy:

> The project that had begun in the eighteenth century as a bid to free every individual from his or her dependence upon the rigid social and

> moral codes by which the powers, secular and religious, of the old regime had kept their subjects in check and to create a fit social world in which all human beings might flourish had, by the twentieth century, evolved into little more than the attempt by a self-convinced European elite to impose its own will and its own image upon the entire world. (15)

From a postmodern perspective, we must respect the values and practices of every culture and society, and so the push for a globalized world can only be a source of oppression. This form of moral relativism prevents us from taking any hard stand on universal human rights because it privileges the particular over the universal.[61] However, since we are seeing both the increase in human lifespans and a decrease in religious authority in the daily lives of people all over the world, then it should be clear that there are moral principles that should be affirmed by all people and cultures. In other words, if we take the extension of lifespans as a founding moral good, then we have to determine what has caused this good to occur, and as Pinker convincingly shows, it is the modern mixture of science, democracy, and capitalism that has been responsible for this progress, and these modern institutions can be traced back to the necessary but impossible Enlightenment ideals of universality, empiricism, and objectivity.

Promoting Modernity

Our world, therefore, has been improved by a group of ideas that have restructured our lives and have countered a set of conservative ideals centered on the premodern conservation of social hierarchies through faith, fate, and belief. Thus, instead of seeing reason as a Eurocentric form of tyranny, we need to think of this way of thinking as the surest path for global human progress. Turning to Kant, Pagden seeks to define the Enlightenment as a new mode of society centered on freeing individuals from premodern social hierarchies: "It was, as Kant argued in the most famous of the many replies that Zöllner received to his troubling question, reason that would allow the still infantile person to exit from its 'self-incurred minority'" (16). Just as Freud posits that humans develop by replacing their dependency on others with the freedom of their own thought and speech, Kant believed that the key to social progress was the autonomy of thought, but we should not confuse this promotion of free thinking with the libertarian backlash against society.[62] Instead, for Kant, individual freedom is protected by universal social laws and norms that are the result of human intervention and not some natural or divine order.[63]

Of course, a limitation of Kant's own thought is that he excluded certain groups, like women, from being part of the universal law, yet, his philosophy has helped to build a social system that transcends the premodern investment in prejudice, predetermination, and a naturalized social order.[64]

Similar to the way Descartes places doubt at the heart of science, Kant realized that the only way for people to pursue reason was for them to question all previous knowledge and authority:

> Enlightenment would allow the individual to walk by himself. It would liberate him (and increasingly her) from the constraints that had been placed upon him. But to achieve this end, he had to question what his pastor, his doctor, the books he had read, even his ruler had to say. (16)

I have tied this process of enlightenment to psychoanalysis because at the center of analytic practice is the principle of free association, which tells the patient to say whatever comes to his or her mind without any type of judgment.[65] By speaking without censoring, one learns how to suspend one's dependency on the judgments of others, and this suspension is made possible through the neutrality of the analyst, who must also learn to stop relying on knowledge that is already there.[66] As a bias against bias, modern Enlightenment thus issues in a cultural order where all authorities have to be called into question, and yet people still need something in which to believe.[67] From the perspective of global modernity, individual autonomy must be combined with the acceptance of the ideals of reason, which as I have stressed are necessary but impossible to fully achieve.

As a modern thinker, Freud defined science and the reality principle by the acceptance of the limits of our knowledge.[68] Instead of seeing psychoanalysis as providing a total view of the self and the world, Freud followed Kant in affirming that not everything can be known, and we get in trouble when we believe that total knowledge is possible.[69] The paradox, then, of the Enlightenment is that that a culture focused on knowledge ends up discovering what is unknown and unknowable. Freud called this acceptance of the limits of knowledge, humility, and unlike current evolutionary psychologists and neurosciences, he affirmed that even our own self-knowledge is highly limited.[70] However, our lack of knowledge fuels a desire for more knowledge, and this quest to know the truth drives our science and should be the heart of our educational systems. Sadly, much of the way people are taught today emphasizes the memorization and assessment of knowledge that is already there, and so the desire to know is often effaced.[71] We have therefore created modern institutions that undermine modernity itself.

Throughout this book, I have argued that we need psychoanalysis to understand the main political ideologies, and in the case of what I am calling modern liberal globalism, we see that not only does psychoanalytic theory and practice help us to understand the meaning of reason in our daily lives and social structures, but as Pagden insists, the Enlightenment is itself based on the need to define human nature:

> For at the core of the "Enlightenment project" was an attempt to discover a new definition of nothing less than human nature itself. And this required far more than the simple application of unfettered reason. It required, first, an understanding of the "passions," in particular those passions that in the eighteenth century were referred to as "sentiments." It required a complete revaluation of the sources of human sociability.
>
> (16)

The modern break with the conservative premodern ideology and social hierarchy not only required a new set of social institutions but also a new way of understanding human subjectivity. It turns out that if you want to change the social order, you also have to develop a theory of how the mind works, and psychoanalysis can help us to think about this process since much of our ways of being are unconscious and irrational. Not only is it important to comprehend how reason works in our minds, but we also have to think about emotions, intersubjectivity, and passionate attachments.

Pagden argues that the Enlightenment promotes the idea that our human nature has nothing to do with divinity, and it must be considered to be universal: "The 'science of man' was to be, as the natural sciences had now become, resolutely secular. The second was that there exists a universal 'human nature,' which could be understood wherever it was found" (17). This focus on the universality of the human mind still remains highly controversial because it appears to hide Eurocentrism under the cover of global equality. Just as psychoanalysis has been criticized for not taking into consideration larger social, historical, and cultural factors, it has been argued that the Enlightenment's investment in universality blinds it from seeing important differences.[72] However, I have been arguing that like psychoanalysis, the model of the human mind presented by modernity combines together an understanding of the interaction among nature, culture, and subjectivity through the application of the shared ideals of objectivity and empiricism. It is vital to stress that these ideas create an open system that is constantly being transformed, but its key principles remain intact. For instance, in psychoanalytic practice, each case is unique, but the same technique is applied in most cases, and this technique is derived from a set of universal principles: freedom, neutrality, and introspection.[73] Since the reality principle tells us that our knowledge is always incomplete, and we can never fully escape reality or our own memories, the universal method of free speech results in an acknowledgment of the limits of our knowledge coupled with a desire to know more. Once again, while the process is universal, the experience and content are always unique and singular.

From the perspective of modern democracy, each vote should be equal to the next, and everyone should have equal access to the law through the same due processes and the same equal treatment.[74] What some people on the Left object to this aspect of Enlightenment universality is that the law is never fully equal, and there are always prejudices and biases shaping the system.[75] I have argued that these biases come from premodern social hierarchies, and it is the desire of modern reason to escape bias through critical introspection, yet, this process does not always work. Likewise, psychoanalysts are supposed to be analyzed, in part, so they can overcome their own bias as they become committed to analytic neutrality. However, some critics of Freud have argued that this notion of neutrality is cold and impersonal and serves to block important social factors.[76] However, what this criticism misses is the idea that psychoanalysis is based on the construction of an artificial social relationship that counters our everyday experience of ourselves and our social worlds. This break from the everyday is necessary because people have to suspend their usual way of seeing themselves and the world around them.[77]

Like psychoanalysis, then, modern democratic reason requires a break from our natural and learned modes of thinking and speaking, and this break is founded on the artificial ideal of neutrality. To be neutral is to treat everything the same without bias, which is the core of universality, equality, and globality.[78] Although impartiality can be accused for being impersonal and indifferent, modern law has actually proven to be the best protection for individual rights.[79] Moreover, the need to provide equal treatment for all people under the law helps to fight against the influence of prejudice, discrimination, and bias, and yet the current backlash against modern democracy continues to come from the Left and the Right. As we have seen, according to the ideology of the Left, the quest for universal human rights continues to fail because there always remain injustices and biases. Likewise, the Right often sees modern institutions as undermining a desire for social hierarchy and a return to a premodern mode of social order. However, since it is impossible to kill an idea, Pagden insists that even with all of the reactions to the Enlightenment project, it continues to expand and shape our world: "Enlightenment was a continual process that might never be completed. But what all those who participated in it were certain of was that it could not now be reversed" (21). Just as our knowledge is never complete, the project of the Enlightenment is never completed, and this makes the universal dynamic and pragmatic. As many commentators have argued, it is rare for a country to go from being a modern democracy to some other non-democratic form, and it is also rare for two democracies to go to war with each other, even though there have been important exceptions.[80] Furthermore, once people have a taste of individual freedom, it is hard for them to go back to a state of enslavement or social control. It is also difficult to repress a new technology or scientific discovery, and so the path of history might not be in a straight line, but it always moves in the same direction.

Pagden highlights how most of the modern revolution has been peaceful and imperceptible even though it did require a series of violent wars between different Christian sects. Once, the hold of Catholic social organization lost its grip, even the growth of non-Catholic forms of Christianity did not lead to the return of theocracies in most parts of the world.[81] However, as Pagden admits, this break with religious determinism did result in a sense of a loss of meaning and purpose for many Europeans:

> Europeans who had once lived in a world of theological certainty and who had, at least at the level of belief, all shared a common culture now found themselves adrift. And since theology had provided the basis not only of their understanding of their relationship with God but also of their moral and even their physical worlds, they were driven to reexamine not merely all the old certainties but, more significantly, all the older methods of inquiry.
>
> (30)

From a conservative ideological perspective, modernity is a destructive force because it removes the source of meaning and purpose from people's lives, and yet, we have seen that what the Enlightenment brings is the combination of individual freedom and a new set of democratic and scientific values centered on equality and neutrality. One problem is that we rarely see science as having a set of moral ideals, and so it is easy to see reason as a meaningless social force. It is also important to emphasize that when people are taught to question all prejudices and authorities, they may at first feel lost and full of anxiety.[82] There is also a risk that the ethic of doubt will spread to science itself, and so we have to understand that with the reality principle and the scientific method, doubt is coupled with empiricism and the use of shared methods and concepts of analysis.

The Reason of Unreason

One of the paradoxes that Freud discovered in relation to free association was that even when you tell people to just say whatever comes into their mind, their thoughts do follow a specific logical order.[83] Likewise, when Freud studied irrational human thoughts, he was always quick to show that there was a reason to the unreason, and therefore, even when we are the most free from social constraint, our thinking does follow certain laws and patterns.[84] Since our mind is structured by a network of memories, the movement between our thoughts travels according to specific connections and possibilities.[85] Through psychoanalytic treatment, we discover that we are both free and determined by relationships we cannot control. Central to this type of enlightenment is the acceptance that we will always have to deal with the conflict between freedom and predetermination, and so there is no reason to try to escape this inevitable tension.

Even though psychoanalysis is a modern discourse based on universal reason, it has often been attacked for not being scientific.[86] One possible reason for this dismissal of psychoanalytic practice and theory is that people misunderstand the core aspects of science itself. Through its combination of neutrality, empiricism, transparency, and critical introspection, science should be thought of as the application of the reality principle to all aspects of the self and society. Although some people would like to separate the humanities from the sciences in an effort to base our understanding of humans on biological determinism, I have argued here that the humanities and psychoanalysis help us to see the ways our world is shaped by certain moral ideals, which often function without our conscious awareness.

Since global progress often happens behind our backs, it is easy to take it for granted and not to think about the ideals shaping this belief system. However, as I have argued throughout this book, we need to defend modern reason by understanding the psychopathology of everyday political ideologies. If we do not understand the ways people react to universal human rights, then we will be unable to sustain our move to a more perfect social organization. Of course, true perfection will never be achieved, but this lack of achievement fuels our desire for more enlightenment.

Notes

1 Pagden, Anthony. *The enlightenment: And why it still matters*. Oxford University Press, 2013.
2 Taylor, Charles. *The malaise of modernity*. House of Anansi, 1991.
3 Rozin, Paul. "The weirdest people in the world are a harbinger of the future of the world." *Behavioral and Brain Sciences* 33.2–3 (2010): 108.
4 Williams, David. *Condorcet and modernity*. Cambridge University Press, 2004.
5 Appadurai, Arjun. *Modernity al large: Cultural dimensions of globalization*. Vol. 1. University of Minnesota Press, 1996.
6 Taylor, Charles. "Two theories of modernity." *Public Culture* 11 (1999): 153–174.
7 Pinker, Steven. *Enlightenment now: The case for reason, science, humanism, and progress*. Penguin, 2018.
8 Hallin, Daniel C., and Paolo Mancini. "Americanization, globalization, and secularization" *Comparing Political Communication*. Ed. F. Esser: Cambridge: Cambridge U. Press, 2004: 25–44.
9 Luhmann, Niklas. "The autopoiesis of social systems." *Sociocybernetic Paradoxes* 6.2 (1986): 172–192.
10 Snedeker, George. "Defending the enlightenment: Jürgen Habermas and the theory of communicative reason." *Dialectical Anthropology* 25.3–4 (2000): 239–253.
11 Nicholls, William, ed. *Modernity and religion*. Vol. 19. Wilfrid Laurier University Press, 1987.
12 Schapiro, J. Salwyn. "Condorcet and the rise of liberalism." Studies in Philosophy and Social Science. 4:292. (1934).
13 Mondon, Aurelien, and Aaron Winter. *Reactionary democracy: How racism and the populist far right became mainstream*. Verso Books, 2020.
14 Weitzer, Ronald, and Charis E. Kubrin. "Breaking news: How local TV news and real-world conditions affect fear of crime." *Justice Quarterly* 21.3 (2004): 497–520.
15 Laudan, Larry. *Progress and its problems: Towards a theory of scientific growth*. Vol. 282. University of California Press, 1978.
16 Houvouras, Shannon, and J. Scott Carter. "The F word: College students' definitions of a feminist." *Sociological Forum* 23.2. Blackwell Publishing Ltd, 2008.
17 Kitch, Sally L. "How can humanities interventions promote progress in the environmental sciences?" *Humanities* 6.4 (2017): 76.
18 Porter, Roy. "*The enlightenment*. London: Palgrave, 1990, 1–11.
19 Freud, Sigmund. "Formulations on the two principles of mental functioning." *The standard edition of the complete psychological works of Sigmund Freud, volume XII (1911–1913): The case of Schreber, papers on technique and other works*. Eds. James Strachey and Anna Freud. London; Hogarth (1958), 213–226.
20 Ogden, Thomas H. "On three forms of thinking: Magical thinking, dream thinking, and transformative thinking." *The Psychoanalytic Quarterly* 79.2 (2010): 317–347.

21 Freud, Sigmund. "Negation." In *Organization and pathology of thought: Selected sources*. Ed. David Rapaport. Columbia University Press 1951, 338–348.
22 Leider, Robert J. "Analytic neutrality—a historical review." *Psychoanalytic Inquiry* 3.4 (1983): 665–674.
23 Freud, Sigmund, and A. J. Cronin. *The interpretation of dreams*. Read Books Ltd, 2013.
24 Heimann, Paula. "On counter-transference." *International Journal of Psycho-Analysis* 31 (1950): 81–84.
25 Freud, Sigmund. "The dynamics of transference." *The standard edition of the complete psychological works of Sigmund Freud, Volume XII (1911–1913): The case of Schreber, papers on technique and other works*. Eds. James Strachey and Anna Freud. London: Hogarth Press (1958), 97–108.
26 Stiglitz, Joseph E. *Globalization and its discontents*. Vol. 500. Norton, 2002.
27 Maguire, Steve, and Cynthia Hardy. "The emergence of new global institutions: A discursive perspective." *Organization Studies* 27.1 (2006): 7–29.
28 Robinson, William I. "Theories of globalization." In G. Ritzer*The Blackwell companion to globalization*. Oxford: Blackwell (2007), 125–143.
29 Pinker, Steven. *Enlightenment now: The case for reason, science, humanism, and progress*. Penguin, 2018.
30 Cresswell, Tim. *On the move: Mobility in the modern western world*. Taylor & Francis, 2006.
31 Marx, Karl, and Friedrich Engels. *The communist manifesto*. Penguin, 2002.
32 Wagner, Peter. "Modernity, capitalism and critique." *Thesis Eleven* 66.1 (2001): 1–31.
33 Eagleton, Terry. *Ideology*. Routledge, 2014.
34 Sluhovsky, Moshe. "Discernment of difference, the introspective subject, and the birth of modernity." *Journal of Medieval and Early Modern Studies* 36.1 (2006): 169–200.
35 Solum, Lawrence Byard. "Freedom of communicative action: A theory of the first amendment freedom of speech." *Northwestern University Law Review* 83 (1988): 54.
36 Oryan, Shlomit, and John Gastil. "Democratic parenting: Paradoxical messages in democratic parent education theories." *International Review of Education* 59.1 (2013): 113–129.
37 Freud, Sigmund. *Civilization and its discontents*. Broadview Press, 2015.
38 Brenner, Charles. "The mind as conflict and compromise formation." *Journal of Clinical Psychoanalysis* 3.4 (1994): 473–488.
39 Freire, Paulo. *Education for critical consciousness*. Vol. 1. Bloomsbury Publishing, 1973.
40 Lukianoff, Greg, and Jonathan Haidt. "The coddling of the American mind." *The Atlantic* 316.2 (2015): 42–52.
41 Samuels, Robert. *Teaching writing, rhetoric, and reason at the Globalizing University*. Routledge, 2020.
42 Samuels, Robert. *Teaching the rhetoric of resistance: The popular holocaust and social change in a post-9/11 world*. Springer, 2007.

43 Gannon, Linda. "A critique of evolutionary psychology." *Psychology, Evolution & Gender* 4.2 (2002): 173–218.
44 McGilchrist, Iain. *The master and his emissary: The divided brain and the making of the western world*. Yale University Press, 2019.
45 Raj, Kapil. *Relocating modern science*. Permanent Black, 2006.
46 Schmitt, Carl. *Political romanticism*. Routledge, 2017.
47 Ingram, David. *Habermas and the dialectic of reason*. Yale University Press, 1987.
48 Burks, Arthur W. "Peirce's evolutionary pragmatic idealism." *Synthese* 106.3 (1996): 323–372.
49 Epstein, Charlotte. "The productive force of the negative and the desire for recognition: Lessons from Hegel and Lacan." *Review of International Studies* 44.5 (2018): 805–828.
50 Horkheimer, Max, Theodor W. Adorno, and Gunzelin Noeri. *Dialectic of enlightenment*. Stanford University Press, 2002.
51 Donnelly, Jack. *Universal human rights in theory and practice*. Cornell University Press, 2013.
52 Long, Scott. "Anatomy of a backlash: Sexuality and the "cultural" war on human rights." *New York: Human Rights Watch* (2005).
53 Featherstone, Mike, ed. *Global culture: Nationalism, globalization and modernity*. Vol. 2. Sage, 1990.
54 Makdisi, Saree. *Romantic imperialism: Universal empire and the culture of modernity*. No. 27. Cambridge University Press, 1998.
55 Seth, Vanita. "The origins of racism: A critique of the history of ideas." *History and Theory* 59.3 (2020): 343–368.
56 Pinker, Steven. *Enlightenment now: The case for reason, science, humanism, and progress*. Penguin, 2018.
57 Ridley, Matt. "The rational optimist: How prosperity evolves." *Brock Education: A Journal of Educational Research and Practice* 21.2 (2012): 103-106
58 Powell, Jason L. "Globalization and modernity." *International Letters of Social and Humanistic Sciences* 17 (2014): 1–60.
59 Samuels, Robert. *Zizek and the rhetorical unconscious*. Palgrave Macmillan, 2020, 33–47.
60 Pinker, Steven. *The better angels of our nature: Why violence has declined*. Penguin Group, 2012.
61 Allen, Amy. *The end of progress: Decolonizing the normative foundations of critical theory*. Columbia University Press, 2016.
62 Guyer, Paul. "Kant on the theory and practice of autonomy." *Social Philosophy & Policy* 20.2 (2003): 70.
63 Cheah, Pheng. *Inhuman conditions: On cosmopolitanism and human rights*. Harvard University Press, 2006.
64 Bernasconi, Robert. "Kant as an unfamiliar source of racism." *Philosophers on race: Critical essays*. Eds. Julie Ward and Tommy Lott. Malden: Blackwell (2002), 145–166.
65 Samuels, Robert. *Psychoanalyzing the left and right after Donald Trump: Conservatism, liberalism, and neoliberal populisms*. Springer, 2016.

66 Hoffer, Axel. "Toward a definition of psychoanalytic neutrality." *Journal of the American Psychoanalytic Association* 33.4 (1985): 771–795.
67 Campbell, Mary B., et al. "Enlightenment now: Concluding reflections on knowledge and belief." *Common Knowledge* 13.2 (2007): 429–450.
68 Samuels, Robert. "*Freud for the twenty-first century*. Palgrave Pivot, 2019, 5–16.
69 Freud, Sigmund, and Anna Freud. *Totem and Taboo and other works*. Vol. 13. Random House, 2001.
70 Gantt, W. Horsley. "On humility in science." *Integrative Physiological and Behavioral Science* 26.4 (1991): 335–338.
71 Kohn, Alfie. *What does it mean to be well educated? And more essays on standards, grading, and other follies*. Beacon Press, 2004.
72 Frosh, Stephen. "Psychoanalysis, colonialism, racism." *Journal of Theoretical and Philosophical Psychology* 33.3 (2013): 141.
73 Coward, Rosalind. "On the universality of the Oedipus complex: Debates on sexual divisions in psychoanalysis and anthropology." *Critique of Anthropology* 4.15 (1980): 5–28.
74 Post, Robert. "Democracy and equality." *The Annals of the American Academy of Political and Social Science* 603.1 (2006): 24–36.
75 Skolnick, Jerome H. *Justice without trial: Law enforcement in democratic society*. Quid Pro Books, 2011.
76 Renik, Owen. "The perils of neutrality." *The Psychoanalytic Quarterly* 65.3 (1996): 495–517.
77 Hoffer, Axel, and Virginia R. Youngren. "Is free association still at the core of psychoanalysis?" *The International Journal of Psychoanalysis* 85.6 (2004): 1489–1492.
78 Larmore, Charles. *The morals of modernity*. Cambridge University Press, 1996.
79 Voeten, Erik. "The impartiality of international judges: Evidence from the European Court of Human Rights." *American Political Science Review* V. 102 (2008): 417–433.
80 Weart, Spencer R. *Never at war: Why democracies will not fight one another*. Yale University Press, 1998.
81 Voye, Liliane. "Secularization in a context of advanced modernity." *Sociology of Religion* 60.3 (1999): 275–288.
82 Fromm, Erich. *Escape from freedom*. Macmillan, 1994.
83 Alexander, Franz. "Our age of unreason: a study of the irrational forces in social life." (1942).
84 Gellner, Ernest. *The psychoanalytic movement: The cunning of unreason*. John Wiley & Sons, 2008.
85 Freud, Sigmund. "Project for a scientific psychology (1950 [1895])." *The standard edition of the complete psychological works of Sigmund Freud, volume I (1886–1899): Pre-psycho-analytic publications and unpublished drafts*. Eds. James Strachey and Anna Freud. London: Hogarth (1966), 281–391.
86 Wallerstein, Roberts. "Psychoanalysis as a science: A response to the new challenges." *The Psychoanalytic Quarterly* 55.3 (1986): 414–451.

7 Conclusion

Throughout this work, I have returned to Lacan's interpretation of Freud's theory in order to present a systemic understanding of the ways different political ideologies relate to each other. On the most basic level, this structure helps us to understand how the premodern conservative protection of cultural ideals through an investment in faith, fate, and hierarchy was undermined by the modern focus on reason, universality, empiricism, and neutrality. From a psychoanalytic perspective, this history represents the gradual replacement of the ego-ideal with the reality-testing ego. However, since this process of Enlightenment is never complete, we are still dealing with the ongoing conflict between premodern social hierarchy and the modern quest for universality and individual autonomy.

One way then of understanding the contemporary postmodern Left is to realize that it is driven by minority-based (women, people of color, LGBTQ social movements seeking to reverse premodern hierarchies and realize the goal of modern universal human rights. The central way that these postmodern protests and resistances respond to injustice and inequality is by identifying with the censoring and shaming super-ego: thus, in order to promote progressive social change, progressive social movements try to get others to feel guilty, ashamed, and responsible for exploitation, abuse, and inequality. In turn, the contemporary Right is driven to defend their fantasy of total freedom and enjoyment, and so they perceive the politically correct Leftist super-ego as a form of castration threatening to limit and control their impulsive ids. On a schematic level, we can understand this structure in the following way:

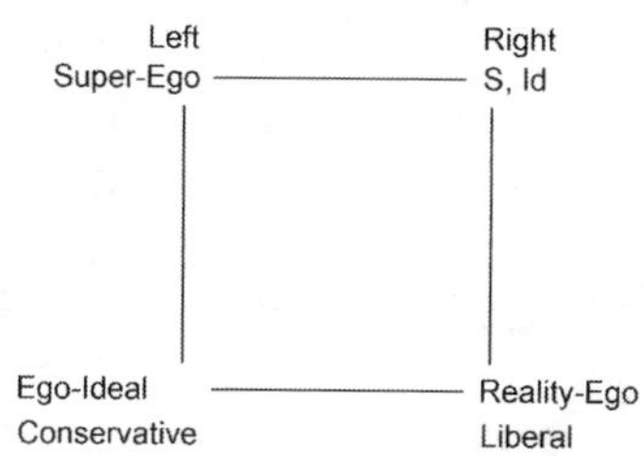

DOI: 10.4324/9781003199649-7

In re-purposing Lacan's Schema L, I have focused on how the Leftist super-ego is in a conflicted relationship with the Right-wing id, while the conservative ego-ideal is countered by the modern liberal reality-testing ego.[1]

An additional aspect of my argument has been that moderate, centrist ideology is structured by an obsessional and narcissistic need to repress conflict and to signal one's virtue to others.[2] This new form of liberalism should be placed in the middle of the previous diagram because it is centered on overcoming the difference between the premodern hierarchy and modern equality through a double alienation where one becomes an other for the social Other:[3]

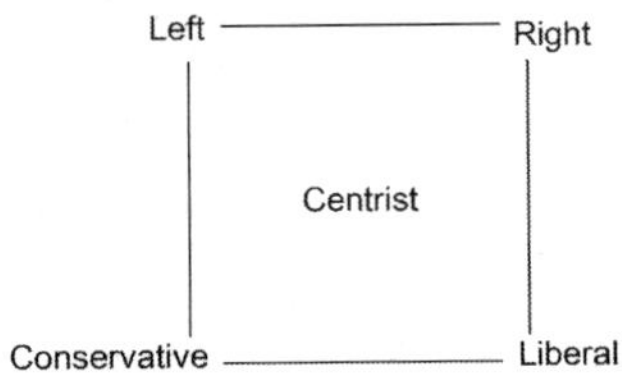

On one level, we can think of these middle-ground moderates as trying to find a compromise solution to the conflicts generated by the opposition between the other ideologies. For instance, someone like Joe Biden likes to preach a message of unity and bi-partisan negotiation. However, on another level, it is essential to point out that this desire for harmony is often driven by the repression of conflict and the presentation of a false ideal self-recognized by a false imaginary other. Since two wrongs do not make a right, when you try to combine two opposed ideological distortions, what you often end up with is a lost ability to address reality in an impartial and empirical way.

Instead of the liberal center being the ideology of science and democracy, it often ends up catering to the demand to have others recognize one as being good, innocent, and knowing.[4] This demand for recognition ends up repressing feelings of guilt, shame, and responsibility as one engages in a public display of morality in order to prove to oneself and others that one is full of good intentions. Thus, one reason why people on the Right often see centrist liberals as being hypocritical, fake, and patronizing is that the centrist ideology is driven by the imaginary relation between an ideal ego and an ideal Other.[5] This double idealization represents an escape from reality through the repression of conflict, guilt, shame, and individual responsibility. However, as psychoanalysis teaches us, we can never fully escape reality or the return of our own thoughts, feelings, memories, and impulses. Since the repressed always returns, the moderate centrists are doomed to repeat the same missed encounter between truth and justice.[6]

It is my hope that this understanding of the psychopathology of political ideologies will help us move to a more rational and universal model of politics. This transformation is necessary because, in order to fight global problems like pandemics, climate change, and financial panics, it is vital to turn to the modern Enlightenment and an understanding of human subjectivity based on psychoanalysis. Instead of repressing our conflicts and signaling our virtues, we have to perceive empirical reality with an open mind and a willingness to be corrected. We also have to stop relying on faith and fate or some higher power to resolve our conflicts as we work through our transferences and idealizations. Rather than pursuing our own pleasure and escaping from difficult problems, we need to give up the fantasies of unlimited enjoyment and freedom. This process also entails breaking with the polarized structure of the innocent victim opposed by the evil perpetrator. While we should not deny the importance of countering all forms of exploitation and abuse, we have to resist the temptation of using suffering as the justification for vengeful aggression. These changes in our politics will only occur if we not only understand the unconscious processes shaping our ideologies, but we also need to act by giving up our passionate attachments to destructive impulses.

Notes

1 Lacan, Jacques. "On the possible treatment of psychosis." *Écrits: A selection* (1959).
2 Saltman, Kenneth J. "'Privilege-checking,' 'virtue-signaling,' and 'safe spaces': What happens when cultural politics is privatized and the body replaces argument." *symplokē* 26.1–2 (2017): 403–409.
3 Samuels, Robert. "Transference and narcissism." *Freud for the twenty-first century*. Palgrave Pivot, 2019, 43–51.
4 Lander, Christian. *Stuff white people like: A definitive guide to the unique taste of millions*. Random House, 2008.
5 Lacan, Jacques. "The mirror stage as formative of the function of the I as revealed in psychoanalytic experience." *Reading French Psychoanalysis* (1949): 119–126.
6 Freud, Sigmund. "Repression." *The Psychoanalytic Review (1913–1957)* 9 (1922): 444.

Index

Made in the USA
Monee, IL
13 September 2026

62977687R00070